Enrico Norelli
Markion und der biblische Kanon

Averil Cameron
Christian Literature and Christian History

Hans-Lietzmann-Vorlesungen

Herausgegeben von
Christoph Markschies

Heft 11/15

Enrico Norelli
Markion und der biblische Kanon

Averil Cameron
Christian Literature and Christian History

DE GRUYTER

Akademieunternehmen „Die alexandrinische und antiochenische Bibelexegese
in der Spätantike – Griechische Christliche Schriftsteller" der Berlin-Brandenburgischen
Akademie der Wissenschaften

ISBN 978-3-11-037405-6
e-ISBN (PDF) 978-3-11-043138-4
e-ISBN (EPUB) 978-3-11-043147-6
ISSN 1861-6011

Library of Congress Cataloging-in-Publication Data
A CIP catalog record for this book has been applied for at the Library of Congress.

Bibliografische Information der Deutschen Nationalbibliothek
Die Deutsche Nationalbibliothek verzeichnet diese Publikation in der Deutschen National
bibliografie; detaillierte bibliografische Daten sind im Internet über
http://dnb.dnb.de abrufbar.

© 2016 Walter de Gruyter GmbH, Berlin/Boston
Druck und Bindung: CPI books GmbH, Leck
♾ Gedruckt auf säurefreiem Papier
Printed in Germany

www.degruyter.com

Vorwort

Mit den Hans-Lietzmann-Vorlesungen erinnern die Berlin-Brandenburgische Akademie und die Humboldt-Universität zu Berlin an einen maßstabsetzenden Historiker des antiken Christentums, an *Hans Lietzmann*. Lietzmann wechselte 1924 von Jena an die Theologische Fakultät der damaligen Friedrich-Wilhelms-Universität, wurde 1926 ordentliches Mitglied der damaligen preußischen Akademie der Wissenschaften und stand dem Akademieunternehmen „Griechische Christliche Schriftsteller", wiederum als Nachfolger Harnacks, seit 1930 vor. Mit der Benennung dieser seit 1995 zuerst nur an Lietzmanns einstigem Wirkungsort Jena, seit 2000 in Jena und Berlin veranstalteten Vorlesungsreihe soll nicht einfach nur an irgendeinen längst verstorbenen Gelehrten erinnert werden, der in Akademie und Universität bedeutende Akzente gesetzt hat, die bis heute fortwirken, beispielsweise im Langzeitvorhaben „Die alexandrinische und antiochenische Exegese" des Akademienprogramms des Bundes und der Länder: Dieses Unternehmen steht in der Tradition des Vorhabens „Die Griechischen Christlichen Schriftsteller", dessen Leiter Lietzmann, wie gesagt, seit 1930 und bis zu seinem frühen Tode 1942 war[2]. Mit diesen Hans-Lietzmann-Vorlesungen soll vor allem an eine bestimmte Art und Weise erinnert werden, die Geschichte des antiken Christentums zu betreiben – eine Form, die nichts an Aktualität eingebüßt hat: Die interdisziplinäre Weite, in der Lietzmann die Geschichte der Antike erforschte, seine selbstverständliche Integration von philologischen, historischen, archäologischen und liturgischen Fragestellungen, war seinerzeit schon etwas Besonderes und ist seither, allzumal angesichts der perniziösen Spezialisierung der einzelnen Wissenschaften, nicht mehr oft erreicht worden. Erst in den letzten Jahrzehnten etabliert sich wieder eine interdisziplinäre Erforschung der Spätantike, übrigens auch und gerade in Berlin – und da lag es vor nunmehr achtzehn Jahren nahe, Lietzmann nicht nur feierlich zum Patron einer solchen Neudefini-

---

[1] Wilhelm Schneemelcher, s.v. „Lietzmann, Hans Karl Alexander (1875–1942)," in: *Theologische Realenzyklopädie* (Berlin/New York: De Gruyter, 1991 = 2000), 21: 191–196; Wolfram Kinzig, „Hans Lietzmann (1875–1942)," in: *Theologie als Vermittlung. Bonner evangelische Theologen des 19. Jahrhunderts im Porträt*, hg. v. Reinhard Schmidt-Rost, Stephan Bitter u. Martin Dutzmann (Arbeiten zur Theologiegeschichte 6; Rheinbach: CMZ-Verlag, 2003), 220–231.

[2] Stefan Rebenich, „Die Altertumswissenschaften und die Kirchenväterkommission an der Akademie: Theodor Mommsen und Adolf Harnack," in: *Die Königlich Preußische Akademie der Wissenschaften zu Berlin im Kaiserreich*, hg. v. Jürgen Kocka unter Mitarbeit v. Rainer Hohlfeld u. Peter Th. Walther (Interdisziplinäre Arbeitsgruppen. Forschungsberichte, hg. v. der Berlin-Brandenburgischen Akademie der Wissenschaften 7; Berlin: Akademie Verlag, 1999), 199–233.

tion und energischen Ausweitung der Antike-Studien auszurufen, sondern darauf aufmerksam zu machen, dass das Rad nicht immer vollkommen neu erfunden werden muss, man vielmehr für eine solche Form der Antike-Studien bei diesem Gelehrten Anregungen bekommen kann. Denn viele einzelne Aspekte, die Lietzmann noch ganz selbstverständlich im Rahmen seiner Forschungen berücksichtigte, sind trotz der gegenwärtig verbreiteten Rhetorik der Interdisziplinarität keineswegs schon wieder und überhaupt selbstverständliche Teilbereiche der Erforschung der Antike.

Leider ist aufgrund eines Wechsels in der Herausgeberschaft und der zeitlichen Beanspruchung des verbleibenden Herausgebers die Reihenfolge der publizierten Vorlesungen etwas durcheinandergeraten[3]: Nachdem im Jahre 2009 die 2007 gehaltene Vorlesung von Hendrik S. Versnel über antike Fluchtafeln erschienen war, folgte 2013 die Lietzmann-Vorlesung des Jahres 2010 über „Kodex und Kanon" von Martin Wallraff. Im vorliegenden Doppelheft sind nun die Vorlesungen von Enrico Norelli und Averil Cameron aus den Jahren 2009 und 2013 zusammengestellt, die dazwischenliegenden Texte folgen ebenfalls unmittelbar[4]. Für die Vorlage beider Vorlesungen in einem einzigen Doppelband sprach vor allem der technische Grund, das Format und den Umfang der bisherigen Hefte einigermaßen beizubehalten. Es wird sich aber, wenn Autor und Autorin – den Usancen der Reihe entsprechend – im Lichte der Forscherpersönlichkeit Hans Lietzmann vorgestellt und gewürdigt worden sind, zeigen, dass sich auch inhaltliche Parallelen zwischen Biographie und Person der Vortragenden zweier Jahre zeigen. Der Beitrag von Averil Cameron wurde in der englischen Sprache belassen, in der er auch vorgetragen wurde; dagegen hat Enrico Norelli seinen Beitrag selbst ins Deutsche übersetzt. Beide Texte wurden noch einmal gründlich in Berlin durchgesehen und die gesamte Publikation dort sorgfältig betreut[5]. Leider hat die längere Verzögerung dazu geführt, dass die in den letzten Jahren seit

---

[3] Eine Aufzählung von Vortragenden und Themen für die Jahre von 1995 an findet sich auf der Homepage der Jenaer Theologischen Fakultät, an der die Vorlesungsreihe begründet wurde: http://www.theologie.uni-jena.de/Lietzmann.html; eine Bibliographie der bislang erschienenen Bände auf der Homepage des Verlages: http://www.degruyter.com/view/serial/16148 (letzte Abfrage: 26.07.2016).
[4] Lediglich die Vorlesung des Jahres 2008 von Stephen Emmel unter dem Titel „Schenute. Ägyptischer Mönch, Kirchenvorsteher, Prophet und Heiliger. Einblicke in die koptische Kirche von gestern und heute" kann aus verschiedenen Gründen leider nicht gedruckt vorgelegt werden.
[5] Für ihre Mithilfe bei der Veröffentlichung der Manuskripte danke ich meinen Assistierenden Marc Bergermann und Emmanuela Grypeou sowie Eva Markschies; an der Korrektur beteiligte sich zeitweilig auch meine heute in Bochum wirkende Kollegin Katharina Greschat, die mich in den Jahren meiner Präsidentschaft dankenswerterweise vertrat.

2009 erschienenen, recht unterschiedlich angelegten großen monografischen Beiträge zu Marcion in dieser Publikation nicht ausdrücklich gewürdigt werden können; Enrico Norelli wird dies an anderer Stelle nachholen.

In gewohnter Weise werden auch in diesem Doppelband die Vortragenden der Vorlesung knapp vorgestellt und ihr Forschungsprofil in einen Zusammenhang mit Lietzmann gebracht, zunächst *Enrico Norelli*.

Angesichts des Forschungsprofils von Hans Lietzmann lag es nahe, zur gleichnamigen Vorlesung Enrico Norelli einzuladen. Norelli wurde 1952 in Grosseto geboren und erwarb einen philosophischen und einen theologischen Doktorgrad an den Universitäten Pisa und Genf. Nach einer Zeit am Istituto per le Scienze religiose Bologna (1975 bis 1982), an der Universitätsbibliothek von Bologna (1977 bis 1989) und an der Universität Triest (1985 bis 1988) wirkt Norelli seit Februar 1988 an der Evangelisch-Theologischen Fakultät der Universität von Genf, zunächst zuständig vor allem für die apokryph gewordene antike christliche Literatur, seit 2004 als Ordinarius für Geschichte der Ursprünge des Christentums. Der Name von Enrico Norelli ist für die meisten, die sich mit dem antiken Christentum beschäftigten, zunächst einmal mit zentralen Editionen verbunden, die alle am Fach Interessierten praktisch jeden Tag nutzen: Bekannt wurde er breiteren Kreisen durch seine Beteiligung an der großen Edition der „Himmelfahrt Jesajas"[6], aber auch durch eine kommentierte und übersetzte Ausgabe der Schrift des Hippolyt über den Antichrist[7] und schließlich eine mustergültige Edition mit Übersetzung und reichem Kommentar der Fragmente des Papias[8]. Daneben stehen verschiedene Studien zur Geschichte der Kanonisierung der christlichen Bibel[9], zur apokryphen Literatur und

---

6 *Ascensio Isaiae, Vol. 1 Textus*, cura Paolo Bettiolo, Alda Giambelluca Kossova, Claudio Leonardi, Enrico Norelli, Lorenzo Perrone (Corpus Christianorum. Series Apocryphorum 7; Turnhout: Brepols, 1995); *Vol. 2 Commentarius*, cura Enrico Norelli (Corpus Christianorum. Series Apocryphorum 8; Turnhout: Brepols, 1995); vgl. auch ders., *L'Ascensione di Isaia. Studi su un apocrifo al crocevia dei cristianesimi* (Collana Origini. Nuova Serie 1; Bologna: Dehoniane, 1994) mit Rezension von Luise Abramowski, *Zeitschrift für Kirchengeschichte* 107 (1996): 432f.
7 *Ippolito, L'Anticristo. De Antichristo*, a cura di Enrico Norelli (Biblioteca Patristica 10; Florenz: Nardini, 1987).
8 *Papia di Hierapolis, Esposizione degli Oracoli del Signore. I frammenti*. Introduzione, testo, traduzione e note di Enrico Norelli (Letture Cristiane del primo millennio 36; Mailand: Paoline, 2005).
9 *Le canon du Nouveau Testament. Regards nouveaux sur l'histoire de sa formation*, sous la direction de Gabriella Aragione, Éric Junod et Enrico Norelli (Le monde de la Bible 54; Genf: Labor et Fides, 2005), von Norelli dort: „Papias de Hiérapolis a-t-il utilisé un recueil 'canonique' des quatre évangiles?," a.a.O. 35–85.

zu Marcion, die hier natürlich nicht alle genannt werden können[10]. Ergebnis langjähriger Beschäftigung mit Themen apokryph gewordener Literatur ist ein gehaltvolles Bändchen zu Vorstellungen und Bildern von Maria in diesen Texten[11]. Damit sind seine Interessen aber keineswegs erschöpft; so verbindet ihn offenbar eine Art verborgene Liebe mit den streng lutherischen Theologen der reformatorischen Zeit[12]. Vielfach bekannt geworden ist Norelli schließlich auch durch eine gemeinsam mit Claudio Moreschini verfasste Literaturgeschichte, die in etliche Sprachen übersetzt wurde[13]; eine knappere Epitome für studentische Zwecke ist übrigens auch in Deutschland erschienen[14]. Ebenfalls für studentische Zwecke bestimmt ist die jüngste Veröffentlichung über die „Geburt des Christentums"[15]. Im Fach gut bekannt ist Norelli auch durch seine engagierte Mitarbeit in der „Association pour l'Étude de la Littérature Apocryphe Chrétienne", die durch die enge Zusammenarbeit der einschlägigen Institute in Genf und Lausanne getragen wird, jedes Jahr spannende Tagungen veranstaltet und ein Bulletin mit wertvoller Bibliographie publiziert[16]. Norelli gibt mit Kollegen die knapp kommentierte, in Taschenbuchform erscheinende Reihe „Apocryphes. Collection de poche de l'AELAC" heraus, in der auf Grundlage der kritischen Ausgaben in der Apokryphen-Serie des Corpus

---

[10] Eine Bibliographie aus dem Jahre 2015 findet sich auf der Homepage von Enrico Norelli (letzter Zugriff am 26.07.2016): https://www.unige.ch/theologie/files/2614/4490/6072/Norelli_publications_2015.pdf.
[11] Enrico Norelli, *Marie des apocryphes. Enquête sur la mère de Jésus dans le christianisme Antique* (Christianismes antiques; Genf: Labor et Fides, 2009).
[12] Enrico Norelli, „L'autorità della chiesa antica nelle Centurie di Magdeburgo e negli 'Annales' del Baronio," in: *Baronio storico e la Controriforma*. Atti del Convegno internazionale di studi, Sora 6-10 ottobre 1979, cura di Romeo De Maio, Fonti e Studi Baroniani (Sora: Centro di Studi Sorani „Vincenzo Patriarca", 1982), 253–307.
[13] Claudio Moreschini, *Storia della letteratura cristiana antica greca e latina Vol I. Da Paolo all'età costantiniana; Vol. II/1–II/2. Dal concilio di Nicea agli inizi del Medioevo*, 2 Vols. in 3 Bänden (Brescia: Morcelliana, 1995–1996).
[14] Claudio Moreschini/Enrico Norelli, *Handbuch der antiken christlichen Literatur*, aus dem Italienischen übersetzt von Elisabeth Steinweg-Fleckner u. Anne Haberkamm (Gütersloh: Gütersloher Verlagshaus, 2007); vgl. die Rezension von Christoph Markschies, *Theologische Literaturzeitung* 134 (2009): 315–317.
[15] Enrico Norelli, *La nascita del cristianesimo* (Le vie della civiltà; Bologna: Società editrice il Mulino, 2014), französisch: *Comment tout a commencé. La naissance du christianisme*, traduction française par Viviane Dutaut (Paris, Bayard, 2015).
[16] https://wp.unil.ch/aelac/ (letzte Abfrage 26.07.2016).

Christianorum viele Texte erstmals mit einer vorzüglichen Übersetzung erscheinen, inzwischen außer in französischer auch in englischer Sprache[17]. Es ist sicher nicht übertrieben, Norelli als einen Brückenbauer zwischen der ungeheuer produktiven italienischen Kunde des antiken Christentums und Patristik und den französischen sowie deutschen Initiativen auf diesem Gebiet zu bezeichnen. Durch seine besondere Liebenswürdigkeit, die sich mit großer Sensibilität für Texte und exegetischer Gründlichkeit paart, ist er für eine solche Funktion als Brückenbauer auch besonders disponiert.

Zu *Hans Lietzmann*, der der Vorlesung den Namen gegeben hat, lassen sich vielerlei Linien ziehen. Da ist natürlich *zuerst* die große Darstellung der Kirchengeschichte[18], die Lietzmann allerdings in späteren Jahren gleichsam als Summe seiner Beschäftigung mit dem antiken Christentum schrieb – Norelli hat mit dem Abfassen von Lehrbüchern deutlich früher begonnen. Ein *zweiter Punkt*, der Norelli und Hans Lietzmann verbindet, ist das Interesse für die Kanonisierung des Neuen Testamentes und die Apokryphen[19]. Lietzmann hat zwar nicht viel über die Apokryphen veröffentlicht, aber seinem Schüler Wilhelm Schneemelcher weitergegeben, dass die apokryph gewordenen Texte sehr viel stärker als die normalerweise im Fokus der Forschung stehenden Schriften der „großen Theologen" und „prominenten Bischöfe" die Religiosität breiter Schichten antiker Bevölkerung überliefern und schon deshalb das Studium lohnen. Schneemelcher entschloss sich nach eigenen Aussagen deswegen, ein Angebot anzunehmen, die maßgebliche deutsche Übersetzungssammlung dieser Schriften in revidierter Fassung herauszubringen, und widmete sich dieser Arbeit praktisch sein ganzes Professorenleben bis weit nach der Emeritierung[20]. Ein *drittes gemeinsames Arbeitsfeld* ist die Forschung auf dem Gebiet derjenigen antiken Literatur, die man gewöhnlich der „Gnosis" zuweist. So wie Lietzmann den Luftballon der Mandäer-

---

17 *The Syriac Pseudo-Clementines. An Early Version of the First Christian Novel*, translated into English by F. Stanley Jones (Apocryphes. Collection de poche de l'AELAC 14; Turnhout: Brepols, 2014).
18 Hans Lietzmann, *Geschichte der Alten Kirche*, mit einem Vorwort von Christoph Markschies (De Gruyter Studienbuch, Berlin/New York: De Gruyter, 1999).
19 Einschlägige Studien sind gesammelt in: Hans Lietzmann, *Kleine Schriften, Bd. 2 Studien zum Neuen Testament*, hg. v. Kurt Aland (Texte und Untersuchungen 68; Berlin: Akademie Verlag, 1958).
20 Details und Literatur: Christoph Markschies, „Haupteinleitung," in: *Antike christliche Apokryphen*, 7. Auflage der von Edgar Hennecke begründeten Sammlung, Band 1 *Evangelien und Verwandtes*, hg. v. Christoph Markschies und Jens Schröter in Verbindung mit Andreas Heiser (Tübingen: Mohr Siebeck, 2012), 1–180.

Forschung zerplatzen ließ[21], analysiert Norelli mit großer Sensibilität die Überlieferungen zu Marcion. Das tut angesichts mancher gegenwärtiger Aufgeregtheiten um diesen christlichen Theologen nur gut. Lietzmann hat über Marcion selbst nichts geschrieben; hier hätte er sich viel zu sehr mit der großen Monographie seines Vorgängers Harnack auseinandersetzen müssen, die (jedenfalls aus heutiger Perspektive) mehr über ihren Autor und die Zeitsituation verrät als über einen stadtrömischen Theologen des zweiten Jahrhunderts[22].

Als zweite Autorin dieser Doppelpublikation ist *Averil Cameron* vorzustellen und knapp zu Lietzmann in Beziehung zu setzen. Averil Cameron konnte schon deswegen quasi als eine geborene Vortragende im Rahmen der Hans-Lietzmann-Vorlesungen gelten, weil auch sie (wie der namensgebende Jenaer und Berliner Gelehrte) die Grenzen der klassischen Erforschung der Antike entschlossen ausgeweitet hat.

She has, to move into her English language[23] and cite some words from the introduction of her Festschrift, published in 2007, "expanded the intellectual horizons of successive generations of classical scholars who have come to the realization that the classical world, albeit transformed, is encapsulated in Procopius of Caesarea as much as it is in Herodotus"[24]. Averil Cameron is Professor Emerita of Late Antique and Byzantine History in the University of Oxford, Dame and Fellow of the British Academy and previously Professor at King's College London between 1994 and 2010, she was the Warden of Keble College, Oxford, – one of the few women to head a former men's college at Oxford. She received honorary

---

21 Hans Lietzmann, *Ein Beitrag zur Mandäerfrage*. Sonderausgabe aus den Sitzungsberichten der Preußischen Akademie der Wissenschaften. Philosophisch-historische Klasse 1930 (Berlin: De Gruyter, 1930; mehrfach nachgedruckt); vgl. die Rezension von Rudolf Bultmann, *Theologische Literaturzeitung* 56 (1931): 557–580.
22 Adolf von Harnack, *Marcion: Das Evangelium vom fremden Gott: Eine Monographie zur Geschichte der Grundlegung der katholischen Kirche. Neue Studien zu Marcion* (Texte und Untersuchungen 45 und 44/4. 2., verbesserte und vermehrte Aufl. Leipzig: Hinrichs, 1924 = Darmstadt: Wissenschaftliche Buchgesellschaft, 1960).
23 Mit Rücksicht auf den gewachsenen internationalen Markt erscheint die von Averil Cameron in englischer Sprache gehaltene Vorlesung auch in dieser Form; die bisherige Praxis, englische, französische oder italienische Vorlesungen in die deutsche Sprache zu übersetzen, wird in Zukunft nicht mehr fortgesetzt. Bei meiner Mitarbeiterin Dr. Emmanouela Grypeou möchte ich mich sehr herzlich für die sprachliche wie inhaltliche Zuarbeit zu diesem Abschnitt bedanken, der auch eine Frucht ihrer eigenen Zeiten in Oxford darstellt.
24 Hagit Amirav and Bas ter Haar Romeny, „Preface," in: *From Rome to Constantinople. Studies in Honour of Averil Cameron*, ed. by Hagit Amirav and Bas ter Haar Romeny (Late Antique History and Religion 1; Löwen: Peeters, 2007), (IX–XI) XI.

doctorates in Letters from the Universities of Warwick, St Andrews, Aberdeen, and the Queen's University of Belfast. Averil Cameron is currently chair of the Oxford Centre for Byzantine Research. She wrote once: "I was the only child of working-class parents in the small moorland town of Leek, Staffs. Not surprisingly, I found Oxford in the late 1950s an alarming prospect. (...) ... Arnaldo Momigliano took me on when I eventually arrived in London from Scotland with a half-finished PhD"[25].

Averil Cameron has provided thorough and illuminating studies of the works of – mainstream and not so mainstream – historians, such as Agathias[26] and Procopius[27], and has offered new insights in the assessment and placement of their work but also in the re-evaluation of the corresponding historical eras of the Byzantine world as a whole. Through a detailed attention to the sources she has, further, provided works of breath-taking erudition in the history of the Roman world and the Eastern Mediterranean in Late Antiquity, stressing the significance of the thorough examination of Christian literature in the context of the study of Roman and late antique history. In her most recent monograph, published under the title: "Dialoguing in Late Antiquity" in 2014[28], she challenged long established notions about the end of a culture of "dialogue" among Christians by the fifth century C.E. This work can be regarded as a continuation or "Anknüpfung", to use a German term, of her magisterial work "Christianity and the Rhetoric of the Empire"[29], in which she studied the main elements and the development of the Christian discourse in Late Antiquity in order to explain and analyze Christianity's success in becoming the dominant ideology of the Roman Empire. Furthermore, she is the editor of volumes 12–14 of Cambridge Ancient History[30]. Her volume "The

---

25 Averil Cameron, „Past Masters, in: *Times Higher Education*, 27th October 1994, see https://www.timeshighereducation.com/features/past-masters/154599.article (letzte Abfrage: 29.07.2016).
26 *Agathias* (Oxford: Clarendon Press, 1997).
27 *Procopius and the Sixth Century* (Classical Life and Letters; London: Duckworth, 1985 = Transformation of the Classical Heritage 10; Berkeley and Los Angeles: University of California Press, 1985).
28 *Dialoguing in Late Antiquity* (Hellenic Studies 65; Washington, D.C.: Center for Hellenic Studies, Trustees of Harvard University, 2014).
29 *Christianity and the Rhetoric of Empire: The Development of Christian Discourse* (Berkeley and Los Angeles: University of California Press, 1991).
30 *The Cambridge Ancient History. Vol. 12: The Crisis of Empire AD 193–337* (Cambridge: Cambridge University Press, 1993); *The Cambridge Ancient History. Vol. 13: The Late Empire AD 337–425* (Cambridge: Cambridge University Press, 1997); *The Cambridge Ancient History. Vol. 14: Late Antiquity Empire and Successors AD 425–600* (Cambridge: Cambridge University Press, 2001).

Later Roman Empire" (1993)[31], which mainly focused on the fourth century and largely on Constantinople, was translated by Kai Brodersen into German under the title "Das späte Rom" and published one year later, in 1994[32].

A foremost historian of Late Antiquity, Averil Cameron has contributed major insights into our understanding of Late Antiquity as a historical category per se and has urged a re-thinking of the construction and definition of established interpretations and understanding of traditional historical categories. Her work is characterized by a remarkable range of themes and methodological approaches, applying a rigorous inter-disciplinary approach in most of her work, whereas she has not only questioned but also often transgressed chronological boundaries, and over-turned traditional categories in the context of a critical re-consideration of Late Antiquity. Significantly, she has used sociological and socio-anthropological methodological models on the historical study of the world of Late Antiquity. Notably, as she writes: "the kind of history written depends on the intellectual and educational context, in which it is produced"[33]. Accordingly, the historian becomes part of the written history as well as of the historical investigation.

There are a number of points that exceptionally link Hans Lietzmann with Averil Cameron. *Firstly*, both Cameron and Lietzmann are connected with two giants of the study of early Christian history and namely, Cameron with her mentor, Arnaldo Momigliano and Lietzmann with his predecessor in the Chair of New Testament, Church History and Christian Archaeology at the Faculty of Theology in Berlin, Adolf von Harnack. Notably, both Cameron and Lietzmann are also linked with each other through their respective training in classical philology in young years[34]. In a certain sense they even remained classicists in all their scholarly work and during their long and very productive academic careers. Characteristically, Momigliano "would speak of Averil Cameron, as 'our classical historian'"[35].

---

31 Cameron, *The Later Roman Empire AD 284–430* (Cambridge, Mass.: Harvard University Press, 1993).
32 Cameron, *Das späte Rom* (Antike Geschichte 7; München: Deutscher Taschenbuch Verlag, 1994).
33 Cameron, „The 'long' late antiquity: a late twentieth century model", in *Classics in Progress. Essays on Ancient Greece and Rome*, ed. by T.P. Wiseman (Oxford: Oxford University Press, 2002), (165–192) 190.
34 Wolfram Kinzig, „Hans Lietzmann (1875–1942)," in: *Theologie als Vermittlung. Bonner evangelische Theologen des 19. Jahrhunderts im Porträt*, hg. v. Reinhard Schmidt-Rost, Stephan Bitter u. Martin Dutzmann (Arbeiten zur Theologiegeschichte 6; Rheinbach: cmz, 2003), 220–231.
35 Peter Brown, „Our Debt to Averil Cameron," in: *From Rome to Constantinople. Studies in Honour of Averil Cameron*, (1–10) 3.

In addition, both Lietzmann and Cameron provided outstanding interdisciplinary methodological approaches in their study of Christian history and literature combined with an impressive breadth of research interests. *Secondly*, however, and as already noted, they both moved beyond the strict confines of ancient Christian literature. The work of Averil Cameron on Byzantium, and especially the early Byzantine world, is so well-known and ground-breaking, that there is no need to expand on this here. Hans Lietzmann has also worked on Eastern Rome, and probably, most famously, on Constantine the Great, in the context of his research works on the church and the state in the third century[36]. The figure of Constantine and his imperial as well as his church politics are analysed in an exemplary manner by Averil Cameron in her (co-authored with Stuart G. Hall) introduction and commentary of her translation of Eusebius' The Life of Constantine[37]. An additional, *third*, important point of contact between Averil Cameron and Hans Lietzmann is their interest for asceticism in Late Antiquity. Hans Lietzmann translated into German a number of important ascetic stories, such as the Life of St. Symeon the Stylite[38]. Cameron has demonstrated the crucial impact of the systematisation of asceticism and of the ascetic discourse on the historical formation of Christianity[39]. A *fourth* point to be mentioned is that both scholars expanded in a significant and similar way our understanding of Church History and the history of Christianity in Late Antiquity and beyond. Hans Lietzmann's seminal work, "Geschichte der Alten Kirche", included a magisterial discussion of the Roman Empire as the historical background for his approach to Christian History[40]. Similarly, Averil Cameron, as already noted, co-edited three volumes of the Cambridge Ancient History. Thus, both scholars have produced important historical survey works and offered a comprehensive understanding of ancient Christian history. Still, it is important to note that, as historians (and theologians, as well, in the case of Lietzmann) with a solid classical philological formation, they have not only produced impressive general historical works, but have also

---

36 Hans Lietzmann, *Die Anfänge des Problems Kirche und Staat: Festvortrag in der öffentlichen Sitzung der Preußischen Akademie der Wissenschaften am 27. Januar 1938* (Berlin: De Gruyter, 1938).
37 *Eusebius's Life of Constantine. Introduction, translation and commentary* (Oxford: Oxford University Press, 1999).
38 Hans Lietzmann, *Das Leben des Heiligen Symeon Stylites* (Texte und Untersuchungen 32/4; Leipzig: Hinrichs, 1908).
39 Averil Cameron, „Ascetic Closure and the End of Antiquity", in: *Asceticism*, ed. by Vincent L. Wimbush and Richard Valantasis (Oxford: Oxford University Press, 1995), 145–161.
40 Christoph Markschies, „Vorwort," in: Hans Lietzmann, *Geschichte der Alten Kirche*. Mit einem Vorwort von Christoph Markschies (Berlin/New York: De Gruyter, $^{4/5}$1999), V–XXIII.

provided excellent studies on specific themes, works and authors. For example, one could mention here Lietzmann's study on Apollinaris of Laodicea[41] or his editorial care for the GCS and in the case of Averil Cameron the already mentioned studies and commentaries on Procopius, Eusebius, and Agathias. Accordingly, both scholars combine in all their work a comprehensive historical analysis with an erudite precision and careful attention for the historical and philological detail. A last *fifth* point that needs to be accredited is, that both scholars would impart their deeply learned work on the intricate and complex history and literature of Ancient and Late Antique Christianity in a masterful and captivating for the reader prose.

Am Ende dieses Vorwortes steht wie auch in den voraufgegangenen Heften der Dank. An Averil Cameron und Enrico Norelli dafür, dass sie ihre Manuskripte zur Verfügung gestellt haben und so geduldig auf deren Publikation gewartet haben, an den Verlag De Gruyter und Albrecht Döhnert für ihre Unterstützung der Vorlesung und ihrer Publikation in einem weiteren schön gestalteten Heft dieser Reihe. Die Berlin-Brandenburgische Akademie der Wissenschaften hat erneut die Veranstaltung in ihrem schönen Haus am Gendarmenmarkt beherbergt, auch dafür sei sehr herzlich gedankt.

Neapel, im Sommer 2016   Christoph Markschies

---

41 Hans Lietzmann, *Apollinaris von Laodicea und seine Schule. Texte und Untersuchungen* (Tübingen: J.C.B. Mohr [Paul Siebeck], 1904).

Inhalt

Vorwort —— V

Enrico Norelli
Markion und der biblische Kanon —— 1

Averil Cameron
Christian Literature and Christian History —— 29

Enrico Norelli
Markion und der biblische Kanon*

Das Christentum am Scheideweg im zweiten Jahrhundert

1 Wann „entstand" das Christentum?

Seit langer Zeit wird diskutiert, ob zwischen Jesus und dem Christentum eine Kontinuität besteht. Eine solche Frage mag die Nichtspezialisten überraschen, sie ist aber sehr ernst zu nehmen. Leider – oder, wenn man so will, glücklicherweise – ist die Antwort auf diese Frage heute noch viel schwieriger geworden als je, weil die Problemstellung sich tiefgreifend geändert hat. Denn: was ist eigentlich Christentum? Die Frage, die ich hier stelle, ist weder eine systematische noch eine philosophische, sondern eine historische. Sie lautet, anders gesagt: seit wann ist ein Historiker dazu berechtigt, in der Vergangenheit eine Größe zu identifizieren, die er Christentum nennen darf? Noch komplizierter: wie steht es mit dem Bezug einer solchen Größe zum antiken Judentum? Jeder ernstzunehmende Forscher wird heute erkennen, dass Jesus dem palästinischen Judentum seiner Zeit entstammte. Jeder Forscher wird aber zugleich feststellen, dass nach Jesu Tod einige Gruppen innerhalb des Judentums entstanden sind, die Jesus eine einzigartige und entscheidende Funktion als Mittler zwischen Israel und dem von Israel verehrten Gott zuschrieben. Dies ist an sich noch Judentum. Als Paulus von Tarsus, der im Namen Jesu Christi umherreiste und predigte, schrieb:

> Wir sind zwar von Geburt Juden und nicht Sünder wie die Heiden. Weil wir aber erkannt haben, dass der Mensch nicht durch Werke des Gesetzes gerecht wird, sondern durch den Glauben an Jesus Christus, sind auch wir dazu gekommen, an Christus Jesus zu glauben, damit wir gerecht werden durch den Glauben an Christus, und nicht durch Werke des Gesetzes; denn durch Werke des Gesetzes wird niemand gerecht,[1]

dachte er sicher nicht, dass er sich damit außerhalb des Judentums stellte. Wenn die Apostelgeschichte darin recht hat, dass die Anhänger des getöteten, nachher aber durch Gottes Tat wieder zum (ewigen) Leben gekommenen und dadurch als Messias (Christos) erwiesenen Jesus von Nazareth zum ersten Mal in Antiochien

---
* Frau Professor Katharina Greschat sowie Frau Renate Burri bin ich für die Verbesserung meines deutschen Textes zutiefst dankbar.
1 Galater 2,15–16 (Einheitsübersetzung, 1980).

noch zu Lebzeiten des Paulus als Christen, *christianoi*, bezeichnet wurden (11,26), wird sich Paulus mit mehreren anderen als Christ betrachtet haben.[2] Dies bedeutet aber überhaupt nicht, dass er sich als Glied einer von Israel verschiedenen religiösen Gemeinde sah: *christianoi* konnten sehr gut die Leute sein, die sich innerhalb des Judentums zu Jesus von Nazareth als Messias bekannten.

Sehr schnell aber wurde Jesus, besonders auch durch die Missionstätigkeit des Paulus, als ein solcher Mittler von vielen Leuten erkannt, die nicht Juden waren und von denen jüdische Missionare wie Paulus von Tarsus nicht verlangten, dass sie durch Beschneidung und Beachtung des jüdischen Gesetzes jüdische Proselyten wurden. Andere Anhänger Jesu glaubten indessen, eine Anerkennung Jesu als Messias ohne Eingliederung in das Volk Israel habe eigentlich keinen Sinn. Inzwischen weigerten sich die jüdischen Autoritäten mehr und mehr, besonders nach der Niederschlagung des jüdischen Aufstands gegen Rom, der Zerstörung des Tempels im Jahre 70 und der darauffolgenden tiefen Krise des Judentums, diejenigen Juden als solche anzuerkennen, die an Jesus als den Messias glaubten. Der Grund dafür war, dass Jesus als Mittler bei diesen Juden wichtiger wurde als jenes Gesetz, um das herum die Rabbiner versuchten, das Judentum wieder aufzubauen. Dies wiederum versetzte natürlich jene Juden, die an Jesus glaubten und zugleich das Gesetz weiterhin beachten wollten, in eine äußerst schwierige Lage. Ihre Anzahl verringerte sich; die nichtjüdischen Gläubigen wurden hingegen zur dominierenden Mehrheit. Zugleich waren sie sich aber bewusst, dass die Botschaft Jesu sowie ihr eigener Glaube aus der Religion Israels gewachsen war. Trotzdem war ihr Gottesdienst von dem der jüdischen Gemeinden getrennt und sie wussten, dass das jüdische Volk Jesus als den Messias größtenteils nicht anerkannt hatte. Also: was waren sie? In welcher Beziehung standen sie zur jüdischen Gemeinde auf der einen Seite, zur Mehrheitsgesellschaft auf der anderen, die eng an eine offizielle Religion gebunden war, an der die Christusgläubigen – davon waren jedenfalls wohl die meisten von ihnen überzeugt – nicht teilnehmen konnten, obwohl sie sich in ihrer großen Mehrheit als ein Teil jener Gesellschaft fühlten?

---

2 Vgl. auch Apostelgeschichte 26,28, wo der jüdische König Agrippa dem Paulus spöttelnd erwidert, nachdem dieser ihm erklärt hat, dass die Propheten Israels Jesus als Christus vorausgesagt hatten: „Fast überredest du mich dazu, mich als Christ (*christianos*) auszugeben". Dieses Gespräch ist aber vom Autor der Apostelgeschichte ohne Zweifel lange Zeit nach dem Tod des Paulus verfasst worden.

Dies sind Fragen, die die christlichen Theologen[3] seit dem Ende des ersten Jahrhunderts n. Chr. und das ganze zweite Jahrhundert hindurch intensiv beschäftigten. Wir wissen heute besser als früher, dass ihre Antworten zahlreich und durchaus verschieden waren. Es gibt kein pauschales „christliches Selbstverständnis" bzw. „christliches Selbstbewusstsein". In ihren verschiedenen kulturellen Kontexten und mit ihrem jeweiligen Bildungshintergrund bemühten sich die christlichen Intellektuellen, aber auch die Bischöfe und die Gemeinden insgesamt, mit der geistlichen Tradition der Antike zu interagieren, indem sie die vorhandenen Kategorien und Begriffe aufnahmen und ausarbeiteten. Es handelt sich um äußerst komplizierte Prozesse, umso mehr, weil wir heute besser verstehen, dass es keine Entgegensetzung von „Christentum" einerseits und antiker Bildung oder antiker Gesellschaft andererseits gab.

Wie gesagt, auch die Beziehungen zwischen Christen und Juden sind in jener Zeit nicht als schlichte Entgegensetzung zu verstehen. Vor dreißig Jahren haben die Forscher dies so formuliert, dass das Christentum kein Nachfolger eines schon damals erschöpften Judentums sei (lange Zeit hatten die Theologen von „Spätjudentum" für die Zeit des Urchristentums gesprochen, als ob das Judentum nicht seither weitere zweitausend Jahre gelebt hätte und heute nicht bei ganz guter Gesundheit sei); das Judentum der doppelten Torah habe sich gleichzeitig mit dem Christentum aus dem Judentum des Zweiten Tempels entwickelt; englischsprachige Gelehrte haben gern von „siblings", Geschwistern, gesprochen. Erst damals, so wurde behauptet, fand die „Scheidung der Wege", „the partings of the ways" statt.[4] Heute wird eine solche Vorstellung korrigiert und von „the

---

[3] Über die verschiedenen Typen von christlichen Theologen der ersten christlichen Jahrhunderte und ihre Beziehungen zu den Institutionen im Rahmen des römischen Reiches siehe das umfangreiche Werk von Christoph Markschies, *Kaiserzeitliche christliche Theologie und ihre Institutionen. Prolegomena zu einer Geschichte der antiken christlichen Theologie* (Tübingen: Mohr Siebeck, 2007).

[4] Z. B. James D.G. Dunn, *The Partings of the Ways Between Christianity and Judaism and their Significance for the Character of Christianity* (London: SCM Press; Philadelphia: Trinity Press International, 1991); id. (Hrsg.), *Jews and Christians: the Parting of the Ways, A.D. 70 to 135. Second Durham-Tübingen Research Symposium on Earliest Christianity and Judaism* (Durham, September 1989), Wissenschaftliche Untersuchungen zum Neuen Testament 66 (Tübingen: J.C.B. Mohr, 1992).

ways that never parted" gesprochen: eine Scheidung der Wege habe es nie gegeben, weil Juden und Christen nie aufhörten, aufeinander einzuwirken.[5] Gleichzeitig aber entwickelten christliche Theologen Bilder von „den Juden" bzw „des Judentums", die dazu dienen sollten, christliche Identitäten als Gegenteil dazu zu bilden und zu stärken.[6]

2 Ignatius von Antiochien: *christianismos* gegen *ioudaismos*

Mehrere Antworten wurden auf die Frage nach der Identität des Christentums gegeben: die, die sich schließlich durchsetzte, war, dass es eine kollektive Größe, benannt als *christianismos*, gab – ein Wort, dem man zum ersten Mal, wohl um 115 n.Chr., beim Bischof Ignatius von Antiochien begegnet, – und zwar im Gegensatz zu einem *ioudaismos*. Ignatius schreibt an die christlichen Gemeinden einiger kleinasiatischer Städte:

> „Darum wollen wir, die wir seine Jünger geworden sind, lernen, dem Christentum entsprechend (*kata christianismon*) zu leben" (*An die Magnesier* 10,1);[7] „Es ist nicht am Platz, Christus Jesus zu sagen und jüdisch zu leben (*ioudaïzein*). Denn das Christentum (*christianismos*) ist nicht zum Glauben an das Judentum (*ioudaismos*) gekommen, sondern das Judentum (zum Glauben) an das Christentum" (*An die Magnesier* 10,3); „Wenn euch aber jemand, auf Auslegung gestützt, Judentum verkündigt, den hört nicht an; denn es ist besser, von einem Beschnittenen Christentum zu hören, als von einem Unbeschnittenen Judentum" (*An die Philadelphier* 6,1).

Hier wendet sich Ignatius jedenfalls nicht direkt gegen Juden, sondern gegen Gruppen, die sich als Christen verstehen, die aber Ignatius zufolge in einer Weise

---

5 Siehe besonders Adam H. Becker und Annette Yoshiko Reed, *The Ways That Never Parted. Jews and Christians in Late Antiquity and the Early Middle Ages*, Texts and studies in ancient Judaism 95 (Tübingen: Mohr Siebeck, 2003).
6 Judith M. Lieu, *Image and Reality. The Jews in the World of the Christians in the Second Century* (Edinburgh: T. & T. Clark, 1996); ead., *Neither Jew nor Greek? Constructing Early Christianity, Studies of the New Testament and its World* (London [etc.]: T. & T. Clark, 2002).
7 Die Ignatiusbriefe führe ich an nach der Übersetzung von Henning Paulsen in *Die Apostolischen Väter*. Griechisch-deutsche Parallelausgabe auf der Grundlage der Ausgaben von F. X. Funk/K. Bihlmeyer und M. Whittaker mit Übersetzungen von M. Dibelius und D.-A. Koch, neu übersetzt und herausgegeben von A. Lindemann und H. Paulsen (Tübingen: J.C.B. Mohr [Paul Siebeck], 1992).

leben und denken, die er als jüdisch und insofern gerade nicht christlich brandmarkt. Das Problem besteht darin zu klären, was er unter *christianismos* und *ioudaismos* versteht. Üblicherweise nimmt man an, dass die Leute, gegen die Ignatius sich wendet, an Jesus Christus glaubten, zugleich aber das jüdische Gesetz oder jedenfalls jüdische Bräuche befolgten. Ich denke dagegen, dass Ignatius diese christlichen Gruppen – die seines Erachtens das wahre Menschsein Jesu nicht richtig anerkannten – als Juden „konstruiert", d. h. als Leute, die das Neue am Christentum nicht wirklich erkannt und angenommen haben, um sie zu disqualifizieren.[8] Das Wort *ioudaismos* ist seit dem zweiten Jahrhundert vor Christus bezeugt und drückt eine Behauptung jüdischer Identität besonders in Konfliktsituationen aus, es kann aber verschiedene Nuancen haben und ist keineswegs dem Begriff „Judentum" einfach gleich.[9] Ignatius benutzt es offenbar in negativem Sinn und setzt es dem *a priori* positiven Wort *christianismos* entgegen, das er vielleicht selbst geschaffen hat. Die Kontexte zeigen, dass *christianismos* in den Briefen des Ignatius mit positiven Begriffen wie „Neuheit", „Freiheit" usw. verbunden wird, *ioudaismos* dagegen mit negativen wie „alt", „Knechtschaft" und ähnlichen. Selbstverständlich existierte das Wort *christianos* schon längere Zeit vorher, wie unter anderem die Apostelgeschichte zeigt (s. oben): Das Wort erscheint zwar nicht in den Paulusbriefen, es findet sich dagegen in 1. Petrus 4,16. Was das erste Jahrhundert betrifft, ist jedoch keineswegs klar, dass das Wort die Mitglieder einer als außerhalb des Judentums stehend empfundenen Gruppe bezeichnet. Nach Ignatius dagegen ist der *christianismos* ohne Zweifel dem *ioudaismos* entgegengesetzt und mit ihm unvereinbar; *ioudaismos* meint dann hier offenbar eine Rezeption einer in der Schrift enthaltenen göttlichen Botschaft, die die radikale Neuheit Christi nicht erkennt und sich daher als ganz unzulänglich und rundweg falsch erweist.

Nun besteht kein Zweifel daran, dass der Gott Israels derselbe ist wie der Vater Jesu. Ignatius nimmt an, dass die Juden ihre eigene Heilige Schrift einfach nicht verstanden haben; jedenfalls gibt er in seinen Briefen keine eigentliche Auslegung biblischer Stellen, er lässt im Gegenteil durchblicken, dass er solches nicht gern tun würde, denn die Leute, die er als Häretiker betrachtet, haben ihre

---

8 Enrico Norelli, „Ignazio di Antiochia combatte veramente dei cristiani giudaizzanti?" in *Verus Israel. Nuove prospettive sul giudeocristianesimo. Atti del colloquio di Torino (4–5 novembre 1999)*, hrsg. von Giovanni Filoramo und Claudio Gianotto, Biblioteca di cultura religiosa 65 (Brescia: Paideia, 2001): 220–264.
9 Vgl. Yehoshua Amir, „The Term *Ioudaismos*. A Study in Jewish-Hellenistic Self-Identification", *Immanuel* 14 (1982): 34–41; Shaye J. D. Cohen, „Religion, Ethnicity, and 'Hellenism' in the Emergence of Jewish Identity in Maccabean Palestine" in *Religion and Religious Practice in the Seleucid Kingdom*, hrsg. von Per Bilde [et alii] (Aarhus: Aarhus University Press, 1990): 204–223.

eigenen Auslegungen und bestreiten die des Ignatius (*An die Magnesier* 8,2). Was er jenen entgegenhält, ist, dass seine „Archive" – d. h. ohne Zweifel seine Heilige Schrift – mit Jesus Christus identisch sind; das Evangelium, d. h. die Botschaft Christi, muss das Verständnis der Heiligen Schrift leiten:

> Auch die Propheten aber wollen wir lieben, weil auch ihre Verkündigung auf das Evangelium gerichtet war und sie auf ihn hofften und ihn erwarteten; im Glauben an ihn sind auch sie gerettet worden, in Einheit mit Jesu Christi verbunden, der Liebe und der Bewunderung würdige Heilige, von Jesus Christus bezeugt und dem Evangelium der gemeinsamen Hoffnung zugezählt (*An die Philadelphier* 5,2).

> Denn die Propheten, die Gott besonders nahestanden, haben nach Christus Jesus gelebt. Deshalb sind sie auch verfolgt worden, angeweht von seiner Gnade (*An die Magnesier* 8,2).

Nach dieser Vorstellung ist das Christentum einer Größe, die als *ioudaismos* bezeichnet wird, klar entgegengesetzt, denn beide haben verschiedene Prinzipien; sie haben jedoch zugleich gemeinsame Wurzeln. Dass diese Vorstellung von Ignatius entwickelt wurde, soll übrigens gar nicht bedeuten, dass sie zu dieser Zeit gängig war. Das Christentum wird hier als der allein berechtigte Spross aus jenen Wurzeln betrachtet, während das Judentum daneben nicht das Recht hat zu existieren, denn Gott wollte es durch das Christentum ersetzen. Auf dieses Thema komme ich ganz am Ende meiner Ausführungen zurück.

Zunächst möchte ich die folgende Frage stellen: Was geschieht, wenn man nicht nur „Christ sein" und „Jude sein", sondern auch die Botschaften der Heiligen Schrift Israels und des Evangeliums als unvereinbar ansieht? Wenn man völlig darauf verzichtet, die Bibel Israels in dem Sinne auszulegen, dass sie als an Jesus als dem Christus orientiert erscheint? Wenn man sie als von Gott stammend betrachtet, zugleich aber ihre Aussagen über den Gott, der sich in ihr ausdrückt, ganz ernst und wörtlich nimmt? Was folgt dann daraus für das Verständnis der christlichen Identität? Zweitausend Jahre eines Christentums, das eine Sammlung jüdischer nichtchristlicher Schriften als festen Bestandteil in seine Heiligen Schrift integriert hat, sollten uns nicht vergessen lassen, dass jene andere Möglichkeit wirklich existiert hat. Sie realisierte sich am klarsten und radikalsten mit Markion.

3 Markions Persönlichkeit und Lehre

Über das Leben dieses Mannes, der aus dem Pontus Euxinus im Norden Kleinasiens stammte, sind wir schlecht informiert. Er muss um 140 nach Rom gekommen sein; was über sein Leben vor dieser Zeit überliefert wird, ist feindliche Legende. Aus seinen Schriften ist so gut wie nichts erhalten: unsere Kenntnis seiner Persönlichkeit und seiner Lehre hängt völlig von den Werken ab, die kirchliche Schriftsteller sowohl gegen ihn wie auch gegen eine Menge von Häresien, die sie rekonstruierten und von denen Markions Lehre als eine der gefährlichsten galt, verfasst haben. Dies bedeutet, dass wir die Logik und Kohärenz der Lehre Markions peinlich genau aus Texten wiederherstellen müssen, die Markions Torheit und Widersprüchlichkeit betonen wollen. Hier in der Berlin-Brandenburgischen Akademie der Wissenschaften ist es mir eine Pflicht und zugleich eine Freude daran zu erinnern, dass das bei weitem wichtigste Buch über Markion von einem ihrer großen Mitglieder, Adolf von Harnack, geschrieben wurde. Dieses zunächst im Jahre 1921, dann in zweiter, verbesserter und vermehrter Auflage im Jahre 1924 veröffentlichte Werk ist eines der reizvollsten Bücher des 20. Jahrhunderts im Bereich des antiken Christentums und bleibt trotz aller heute notwendigen Korrekturen der Perspektive *das* unumgängliche Standardwerk zu Markion.[10]

---

10 Adolf von Harnack, *Marcion. Das Evangelium vom fremden Gott. Eine Monographie zur Geschichte der Grundlegung der katholischen Kirche*, 2. Auflage, Texte und Untersuchungen 45 (Leipzig: Hinrichs, 1924), (neuester Nachdruck: Darmstadt: Wissenschaftliche Buchgesellschaft, 1996, mit den Teilen von Harnacks *Neue Studien zu Markion*, Leipzig, 1923, die in die 2. Auflage der Monographie nicht aufgenommen wurden). Die weiteren Gesamtstudien über Markion haben Harnacks Meisterwerk bei weitem nicht ersetzt. Ein wichtiges, aber eher aus Teilstudien zusammengesetztes Buch ist Edwin Cyril Blackman, *Marcion and His Influence*, SPCK (London, 1948), (Nachdruck New York: AMS Press, 1978). Die Monographie von Joseph Hoffmann, *Marcion: On the Restitution of Christianity. An Essay on the Development of Radical Paulinist Theology in the Second Century* (Chico: Scholars Press, 1984) ist ein völlig misslungenes Werk. Die neuere Studie von Sebastian Moll, *The Arch-Heretic Marcion*, WUNT 250 (Tübingen: Mohr Siebeck, 2010), ist eine nützliche Besprechung der meisten Fragen über Markion, der Kern seiner (oft psychologisierenden) Interpretation ist aber m. E. falsch. Moll betrachtet Markion als von einem Fanatismus geblendet, dessen Zentrum der Hass gegen den Schöpfer ist; diese Sichtweise erlaubt nicht, Markions Persönlichkeit wirklich zu verstehen (eine kritische Erörterung dieses Buches findet sich im *Journal of Ecclesiastical History* 61 (2010): 575–576). Gerhard May, *Markion. Gesammelte Aufsätze*, hrsg. von Katharina Greschat und Martin Meiser, Veröffentlichungen des Instituts für europäische Geschichte Mainz 68 (Mainz: Verlag Philipp von Zabern, 2005) ist eine wichtige Sammlung ausgezeichneter Beiträge. Eine gute Zusammenfassung der heutigen Problemstellung gibt Gerhard May und Katharina Greschat (Hrsg.), *Marcion und seine kirchengeschichtliche Wirkung. Marcion and His Impact on Church History. Vorträge der Internationalen Fachkonferenz zu Marcion, gehalten vom 15.–18. August 2001 in Mainz*, TU 150 (Berlin/New York: Walter de Gruyter, 2002). Der französischen Übersetzung von Harnacks *Marcion* (leider ohne die sehr wichtigen Beilagen: *Marcion. L'évangile du Dieu étranger*, Patrimoines christianisme (Paris: Cerf, 2003)) sind einige bedeutende Beiträge von zeitgenössischen Gelehrten hinzugefügt worden, da-

Als Markion in Rom ankam, war er ohne Zweifel schon Christ. Er hatte über die Lehre Christi nachgedacht und sie als radikale Botschaft der Liebe verstanden, einer Liebe, die sich an alle Menschen ohne Unterschied richtet, einschließlich der Fremden und der Feinde.[11] Er hatte begriffen, dass eine solche Haltung

---

runter eine vortreffliche Forschungsgeschichte seit Harnack von Michel Tardieu mit einer äußerst nützlichen Bibliographie: „Marcion depuis Harnack": 419–561. Einen kurzen Überblick kann man auch meinem Kapitel über Markion in Bernard Pouderon (Hrsg.), *Histoire de la littérature grecque chrétienne II, De Paul apôtre à Irénée de Lyon*, (Paris: Cerf, 2013) entnehmen.

11 Markions Schriften besitzen wir leider nicht mehr. Wie wir sehen werden, hatte er eine eigene Rezension der Paulusbriefe und des Lukasevangeliums (das er nicht diesem Verfasser zuschrieb) erarbeitet. Tertullian von Karthago, der in den ersten Jahren des dritten Jahrhunderts (also mehrere Jahren nach Markions Tod) ein fünfbändiges Werk gegen Markion schrieb, benutzte Markions Paulus- und Evangeliumstext, um ihn zu widerlegen. Aus Tertullians *Gegen Markion* und aus einigen späteren antimarkionitischen Schriften, besonders aus dem *Panarion* („Arzneikasten" gegen alle Irrtümer) des Epiphanius, Bischof von Salamis auf der Insel Zypern (um 377), ist es möglich, Markions Text bis zu einem gewissen Punkt wiederherzustellen. Harnacks Versuch (*Marcion*, 67*–240*) ist klassisch geblieben; heute muss man aber auch Kenji Tsutsui, „Das Evangelium Markions: Ein neuer Versuch der Textrekonstruktion", *Annual of the Japanese Biblical Institute* 18 (1992): 67–132 für das Evangelium (nicht immer zuverlässig) und vor allem Ulrich Schmid, *Marcion und sein Apostolos: Rekonstruktion und historische Einordnung der marcionitischen Paulusbriefausgabe*, Arbeiten zur neutestamentlichen Textforschung 25 (Berlin/New York: Walter de Gruyter, 1995) für Paulus (ausgezeichnet) berücksichtigen. John J. Clabeaux, *The Pauline Corpus Which Marcion Used. The Text of the Letters of Paul in the Early Second Century*, Diss. Harvard, Cambridge (MA) (Ann Arbor: UMI, 1989) hat bewiesen, dass mehrere Sonderlesarten in der markionitischen Paulussammlung vor und neben ihm bezeugt sind, so dass sie nicht erst auf Markions theologische Ansichten zurückzuführen sind. Diesem *Instrumentum* hatte Markion die *Antithesen* beigefügt, eine Schrift, deren Gestalt rätselhaft bleibt, die aber folgendes enthalten haben muss: (1) eine wahrscheinlich kommentierte Liste von Antithesen (= Widersprüchen) zwischen Gesetz und Evangelium und deshalb zwischen den Göttern, die nach Markion die Urheber dieser zwei Größen waren (s. unten); (2) eine Skizze der Anfänge des Christentums, die Paulus als den einzigen echten Apostel des Evangeliums Jesu darstellen wollte; (3) eine Erläuterung der Widersprüche innerhalb des kirchlichen Evangeliumstextes, um zu beweisen, dass er interpoliert worden war; (4) Bemerkungen bzw. kurze Kommentierungen zum Text des *Instrumentum*, um ihn im Sinne der markionitischen Theologie zu erklären. Tertullians *Gegen Markion* bildet zugleich unsere Hauptquelle für die Lehre Markions; vor ihm gibt es kurze Nachrichten besonders in einigen Schriften von Justinus dem Märtyrer (um 165: er hatte ein Werk gegen Markion und alle Häresien verfasst, das leider verloren gegangen ist), Irenäus von Lyon (um 190) und Klemens von Alexandrien (um 200), einem Zeitgenossen Tertullians. Die wichtigsten Quellen aus der Zeit nach Tertullian sind die Widerlegung aller Häresien (*Elenchos*), die in Rom zwischen 222 und 235 verfasst wurde, der schon erwähnte Epiphanius, das Gespräch über den richtigen Gottesglauben des „Adamantius" aus dem 4. Jahrhundert, die Widerlegungen des Bardesanes, des Mani und des Markion von Ephrem dem Syrer (gestorben 373) und das armenische Werk *Über Gott* von Eznik von Kołb (um 430).

und Praxis für unsere Menschennatur einfach unmöglich ist; und er war der Überzeugung, dass, die Rettung der Menschen auf eine göttliche Initiative zurückgeht, dieses Eingreifen Gottes etwas bewirken muss, das die Menschen nicht aus eigener Kraft erreichen können, denn sonst wäre Gottes Einschreiten ja überflüssig. Was aber die wichtigste Rolle für Markions Denken gespielt haben muss, ist sehr wahrscheinlich das Empfinden, dass ein menschliches Wesen einfach nicht fähig ist, das Wohl des Anderen, jedes Anderen, vor seine eigenen Interessen zu stellen.[12] Weil nun die Mitte des Evangeliums gerade darin besteht, muss das Evangelium aus einem Anderswo herkommen, das dem Menschen als solchem völlig unvorstellbar ist; dann muss aber das Eingreifen der Gottheit die Menschen auch befähigen, so handeln zu können, wie das Evangelium es fordert, denn ein solches Verhalten ist wider die eigentliche Natur des Menschen.

Wenn aber die menschliche Natur so geschaffen ist, wer hat sie so geschaffen? Markion fand die Antwort fertig vorgebildet in der Offenbarung eines Gottes, der behauptete, die Welt und alles in ihr Enthaltene geschaffen zu haben. Markion musste weder weit entfernt noch lange suchen, denn dies war der Inhalt der Lehre, die er selbst empfangen hatte. Jene Offenbarung findet sich in einer Sammlung von Büchern, in denen der Schöpfergott – Markion nennt ihn mit einem griechischen Wort, welches in der philosophischen, besonders in der platonischen Tradition eine bedeutende Rolle spielt, den Demiurgen – sich dem Volk Israel zu erkennen gibt, nachdem er gerade dieses Volk auserwählt hat, um ihm sein Gesetz aufzuzwingen. Gerade jenes Gesetz sowie die Aussagen der Propheten, durch die der Schöpfer sich ausdrückt, enthüllen die Natur dieses Gottes: er ist begrenzt und unvollkommen, er wird zornig, er will sich selbst und seinen Willen behaupten, er bestraft erbarmungslos die Juden, die ihm nicht gehorchen, er ist nicht allwissend, denn sonst hätte er im Voraus gewusst, dass Adam und Eva ungehorsam sein würden, auch nicht allmächtig, denn sonst hätte er die Menschen so geschaffen, dass sie nicht ungehorsam sein können.

Die Gerechtigkeit bildet nach unseren Quellen die Ureigenschaft dieses Gottes: eine formale Gerechtigkeit, die jedem Menschen Strafe oder Lohn zuteilt, je nachdem, wie er dem Gesetz gehorcht hat. Dennoch ist in den letzten Jahren betont worden, dass die ältesten Quellen über Markion (vor allem Justin um 160 und Irenäus von Lyon um 190, wohl auch der um 170 in Rom entstandene *Brief an Flora* von Ptolemaios) diese Gerechtigkeit des Schöpfers nach Markion in einem

---

12 Enrico Norelli, „Marcion: ein christlicher Philosoph oder ein Christ gegen die Philosophie?", in *Marcion und seine kirchengeschichtliche Wirkung*, hrsg. von May/Greschat (s. oben Anm. 10), 113–130.

eher ungünstigen Licht darstellen: Dieser Gott sei eher selbstsüchtig, machthungrig und böse als wirklich gerecht.[13] Es versteht sich übrigens von selbst, dass ein Gott nicht wirklich gerecht sein kann, der die Menschen in Versuchung führt und sie straft, falls sie das Gesetz übertreten, obwohl sie wegen der Natur, die er ihnen gegeben hat, der Versuchung schwerlich widerstehen können. Außerdem behauptet er: „Ich erschaffe das Unheil" (Jesaja 45,7).

Nach Markions Meinung kann ein solcher Gott einfach nicht der Urheber des Evangeliums sein. Letzteres muss von einem anderen Gott stammen, der mit dem Schöpfer und dessen Schöpfung gar nichts zu tun hat: er ist ihnen eigentlich fremd. Wie der Inhalt des Evangeliums beweist, muss das diesem anderen Gott Eigene die Liebe sein, die das Übel nie wollen kann und deshalb niemanden bestraft. Die Liebe ist daher mit der strafenden Gerechtigkeit schlechthin unvereinbar; diese Anschauung werden die Gegner später Markion vorwerfen, indem sie behaupten, dass ein Gott, der üble Taten nicht bestraft, das Übel nicht ernst nimmt und die Guten nicht schützt. Anders gesagt: ist er nicht gerecht, kann er auch nicht gut sein.[14] Nach Markion muss dieser Gott dem Schöpfer weit überlegen sein, nicht nur weil die Liebe erhabener ist als die Gerechtigkeit, sondern auch und vor allem, weil er selbst bezeugt, dass er von der Existenz eines anderen Gottes keine Ahnung hat. Er behauptet nämlich: „Es gibt keinen Gott außer mir" (Jesaja 45,21 usw.).[15] Der höhere und vollkommene Gott hat seine eigene Schöpfung, die nicht materiell ist, wohl deshalb, weil die Materie nach Markions Meinung zum Bösen neigt.

Während der Demiurg die Welt des guten Gottes überhaupt nicht kennt, sieht der letztere unsere Welt mit ihrem Elend und besonders die Not der Menschen, die unter dem Willen zur Macht ihres Schöpfers leiden. Seiner Güte gemäß wird er vom Mitleid mit ihnen ergriffen und schickt seinen eigenen Sohn in der menschlichen Gestalt Jesu, um den Menschen die Möglichkeit anzukündigen, an die absolute Liebe des Vaters Jesu zu glauben und sich dadurch der Herrschaft ihres Schöpfers zu entziehen, was ihnen eine echte Rettung und Seligkeit beim guten und vollkommenen Gott schenken kann.[16]

---

13 Winrich Löhr, „Did Marcion Distinguish Between a Just God and a Good God?", in *Marcion und seine kirchengeschichtliche Wirkung*, hrsg. von May/Greschat (s. oben Anm. 10), 131–146.
14 Tertullian, *Gegen Markion* 1,26,1–5.
15 Tertullian, *Gegen Markion* 1,11,9; 2,26,1–2.
16 Tertullian, *Gegen Markion* 1,14,2; 1,23,3.

4 Die Schriftensammlung Markions

Woher konnte Markion aber wissen, dass ein solches Verständnis des Evangeliums der echten Botschaft Jesu entsprach? Anders gesagt: wo konnte er die echte Überlieferung Jesu finden? Er war davon überzeugt, dies alles in den Paulusbriefen lesen zu können: er kannte eine Sammlung jener Briefe, die die Pastoralbriefe nicht enthielt – seine Nachfolger scheinen allerdings später auch diese mit hinzugenommen zu haben.[17] Und weil Paulus oft erwähnt, was er „mein Evangelium" nennt, kam Markion zum Schluss, dass solche Erwähnungen auf eine besondere Schrift verwiesen, die die Überlieferung über Jesus enthielt. Aus Gründen, die nicht ganz klar sind, glaubte er, diese Schrift mit einem der umlaufenden Evangelien identifizieren zu können, und zwar mit dem Buch, das als Lukasevangelium bekannt war.[18]

Sowohl die paulinischen Briefe als auch das Lukasevangelium setzen aber offenbar eine aus der Sicht Markions problematische Kontinuität zwischen der Botschaft Jesu und dem Glauben Israels voraus. Nach seiner Auffassung schließen sich diese beiden Größen gegenseitig aus. Wir verstehen Paulus heute so, dass das Evangelium für ihn zur Versöhnung mit Gott genügt; ein an Jesus glaubender Jude

---

[17] Harnack, *Marcion* (s. oben Anm. 10), 132*; Enrico Norelli, „La Lettre aux Laodicéens: essai d'interprétation," *Archivum Bobiense* 23 (2001): 45–90.

[18] John Knox, *Marcion and the New Testament* (Chicago: University of Chicago Press, 1942) hat versucht nachzuweisen, dass Markion nicht die später kanonisch gewordene Gestalt des Lukasevangeliums benutzt habe, sondern einen „Ur-Lukas", den er übrigens verstümmelt habe; dieser Ur-Lukas wäre danach (um 120–125) die Grundlage des „kanonischen" Lukas gewesen, in den mehrere Perikopen, meistens in anti-markionitischer Absicht, eingefügt worden wären. Diese These ist neuestens von Joseph B. Tyson, *Marcion and Luke-Acts. A Defining Struggle* (Columbia, South Carolina: University of South Carolina Press, 2006) weitergeführt worden: Markions Evangelium und der kanonische Lukas seien zwei entgegengesetzte Versuche, das Christentum zu „definieren". Eine Variante dieser Theorie ist von Matthias Klinghardt, „Markion vs. Lukas. Plädoyer für die Wiederaufnahme eines alten Falles," *NTS* 52 (2006): 484–513 entwickelt worden: Markions Evangelium sei (anders als für Knox und Tyson) mit dem „Ur-Lukas" identisch, anders gesagt, Markion habe den existierenden Text ohne Änderungen angenommen; der kanonische Lukas sei, wie für Knox und Tyson, eine erweiterte, antimarkionitische Fassung des „Ur-Lukas". Moll, *The Arch-Heretic Marcion* (s. oben Anm. 10), 90–102, hat das Hauptargument dieser Theorie diskutiert, d. h. die Behauptung, es sei unmöglich, einen Grund für die Tilgung mehrerer Perikopen zu finden, die im kanonischen Lukas, aber nicht bei Markion stehen; Markion habe sie deshalb nicht beseitigt, sondern im „Ur-Lukas" nicht gefunden. Moll zeigt m. E. überzeugend, dass die Entfernung solcher Stücke vor dem Hintergrund der Theologie Markions erklärbar ist. Darüber hinaus denke ich, dass die Beseitigung zumindest einer der zwei Perikopen (von 32), für die Moll keine Erklärung finden konnte, ebenso von Markions Einstellung her verstanden werden kann (s. meine erwähnte Besprechung von Moll).

dennoch das Gesetz weiter befolgen kann, wenn er das will, und eine solche Befolgung keineswegs als zur Rettung notwendig betrachtet wird. Markion verstand Paulus anders: es sei schlicht unmöglich, dem Gesetz und dem Evangelium zugleich zu gehorchen. Die Logik des einen sei nämlich der des anderen entgegengesetzt: das Gesetz sei auf die Selbstbehauptung dessen, der es verkündet, und derer, die ihm gehorchen, gegründet – sowohl auf dem Schutz dessen, der der vom Gesetz bestimmten Gemeinschaft angehört als auch auf der Ausschließung des Fremden; das Evangelium sei dagegen auf der freien Liebe des Anderen und vor allem des Fremden bis hin zum Verzicht auf sich selbst gegründet. Es sei unmöglich, das Evangelium zu praktizieren, ohne das Gesetz zu brechen, und umgekehrt. Jesus habe als erster das Gesetz übertreten. Ein hervorragendes Beispiel solcher Anschauung liefert Markions Auslegung der Heilung des Aussätzigen nach Lukas 5,12–16 (Tertullian, *Gegen Markion* 4,9,3–15, bes. 10). Nachdem Jesus ihn geheilt hat, befiehlt er ihm, vor den Priestern zu erscheinen, wie das Gesetz es verlangt (Leviticus 13,49; 14,2f.). Soll dies bedeuten, dass Jesus von dem Mann die Befolgung eines Gebots des Gesetzes fordert? Keineswegs, antwortet Markion, ganz im Gegenteil. Da Jesus weiß, dass der Aussätzige die Kontrolle der Priester und ein kleines Opfer braucht, um wieder in die Gesellschaft aufgenommen zu werden, schreibt er selbst dem Mann ein solches Vorgehen vor, denn nur so wird der Mann dies tun können, ohne dem Gesetz zu gehorchen und sich dadurch selbst aus der Rettung auszuschließen. Auf diese Weise tut er zwar, was das Gesetz fordert, er tut es aber, weil *Jesus* es ihm befohlen hat.[19]

5 Die Anfänge des Christentums in Markions Sicht

Wie steht es nun aber damit, dass eine positive Wertung des Gottes Israels und seiner Offenbarung sowohl in den Paulusbriefen als auch in dem von Markion akzeptierten Evangelium zu finden ist? Markion erklärte diese Tatsache im Rahmen einer Gesamttheorie der christlichen Anfänge: die von Jesus in einem jüdischen Milieu gewählten bzw. angenommenen Jünger hätten nicht verstanden,

---

[19] Enrico Norelli, „Marcion, Tertullien et le lépreux", in *Nomen latinum. Mélanges de langue, de littérature et de civilisation latines offerts au professeur André Schneider à l'occasion de son départ à la retraite*, hrsg. von Denis Knoepfler, Université de Neuchâtel. Recueil de travaux publiés par la Faculté des lettres 44 (Neuchâtel: Faculté des lettres; Genève: Droz, 1997): 171–180.

dass Jesus einen anderen Gott verkündigte als jenen, den sie kannten. Daher hätten sie nach seinem Tod ein Evangelium verbreitet, das die zwei Götter verwechselte und folglich Jesu Botschaft unnütz machte, anders gesagt, war ihre Überlieferung eigentlich gar kein Evangelium. Jesus habe sich dann aus dem Himmel heraus dem Paulus offenbart und ihn sein Evangelium erkennen lassen; Paulus habe dies getreu verkündet und allen Bemühungen widerstanden, den Gläubigen das Gesetz des Schöpfers aufzuerlegen, wie seine Briefe zeigen. Nach seinem Tod hätten jedoch die Anhänger der Befolgung des Gesetzes sowohl in seine Briefe wie auch in das von ihm inspirierte Evangelienbuch positive Erwähnungen des Schöpfers und der jüdischen Bibel interpoliert[20] und diese Schriften damit verfälscht.

Michel Tardieu ist der Ansicht, dass die Fälschung der Lehre Jesu schon in der apostolischen Zeit und durch die Apostel selbst eine häresiologische Konstruktion Tertullians ist, der sowohl die wahre Lehre wie auch den Irrtum als sehr alt darstellen will;[21] Markion hätte nur die verbreitete Vorstellung der in nachapostolischer Zeit fortschreitenden Korruption der Wahrheit aufgenommen und im Sinne seiner gesamten Anschauung ausgedeutet. Diese These finde ich nicht vollständig überzeugend. Tertullian denkt, dass es Häresien zur Zeit des Apostels gab und dass die späteren Häresien ihre Wurzel in jenen älteren haben (*De praescriptione haereticorum* 33–34). Er betont aber auch, dass der Irrtum notwendigerweise jünger als die Wahrheit sein muss (ebd. 29). Nicht nur an der von Tardieu erwähnten Stelle aus *Adversus Marcionem* 1,21,4 schreibt Tertullian dem Markion die Vorstellung vom Unverständnis der Apostel zu, sondern z.B. auf mehreren Seiten von *De praescriptione* (22–24), wo er auch die alternative (eher von ihm konstruierte) Vorstellung bestreitet, dass die Nachfolger der Apostel die wahre Lehre verfälscht hätten. Darüber hinaus macht Tertullian klar, dass Markion den Konflikt zwischen Paulus und Petrus in Antiochien (Galater 2,11–14) ausgenutzt habe, um zu beweisen, dass Petrus und die anderen Apostel von Paulus als nicht nach der Wahrheit des Evangeliums vorgehend getadelt worden wären.[22] Die anderen Apostel werden im Galaterbrief nicht erwähnt. Es ist gerade

---

20 Für die Quellen vgl. Harnack, *Marcion* (s. oben Anm. 10), 256*–259*. Markions Auslegung von Galater 2,11–21 (sowie von anderen von ihm damit verbundenen paulinischen Stellen) war für seine Rekonstruktion der christlichen Anfänge entscheidend: vgl. Gerhard May, „Der Streit zwischen Petrus und Paulus in Antiochien bei Markion", in ders., *Markion* (s. oben Anm. 10), 35–41; Enrico Norelli, „La funzione di Paolo nel pensiero di Marcione," *Rivista biblica* 34 (1986): 543–597.
21 Tardieu, „Marcion depuis Harnack" (s. oben Anm. 10), 430–432.
22 Siehe besonders *Gegen Markion* 20,2: „Selbst Petrus und die übrigen Säulen des Apostolats, lautet ihr Einwand, wurden von Paulus getadelt, weil sie nicht den richtigen Weg gemäß der

deshalb sehr bedeutend, dass Markion sie hier einsetzt, um zu beweisen, dass alle Apostel außer Paulus das Evangelium entstellt hätten. Mehr noch: in einem 2010 veröffentlichten Beitrag habe ich die Stellen des Evangeliums Markions untersucht, an denen von Jesu Jüngern die Rede ist, und zu zeigen versucht, dass Markion deren Unverständnis der Botschaft Jesu immer wieder betonte.[23] Wenn Markion geglaubt hätte, dass die Jünger Jesu die Botschaft noch originalgetreu wiedergegeben hätten, warum hätte er sich dann darauf beschränkt, nur die Briefe des Paulus wiederherzustellen und nicht auch andere Schriften, die unter apostolischen Namen umliefen, soweit er sie kannte?

Wie dem auch sei: nachdem Markion den Grundsatz des Paulus, d. h. des Evangeliums Christi, erkannt hatte, war er überzeugt, solche verfälschenden Interpolationen entdecken und beseitigen zu können, so dass der Urtext jener Dokumente wiederhergestellt werden könne. So erstellte er das, was Tertullian sein *Instrumentum* nennt, d. h. seine Ausgabe der Paulusbriefe und des Evangeliums, und er fügte die *Antithesen* hinzu, eine Sammlung paralleler Stellen aus der jüdischen Bibel und seinem *Instrumentum*, um zu beweisen, dass die beiden Offenbarungen sich vollkommen widersprechen. Er fügte auch Kommentare zum *Instrumentum* hinzu, die Tertullian bekannt waren. Allerdings ist es schwierig, sich ihre literarische Form vorzustellen.[24]

Eine Position wie die Markions stellt eine radikale Alternative zur damals vorherrschenden Sicht der christlichen Identität sowie der Bedeutung der Tradition und der Kirche dar. Markion durchtrennt jede Bindung zwischen dem Glauben an Jesus und der hebräisch-jüdischen Religion: letztere drückt aus seiner Sicht den Grund des Denkens und des Verhaltens des „natürlichen" Menschen aus, die sich auf eine scheinbar unparteiische Gerechtigkeit stützt, hinter der die Neigung zur Selbstbehauptung und die unvermeidbare Unterdrückung des Mitmenschen stehen. Das Evangelium Jesu ist dagegen „neu", ganz jenseits der menschlichen Möglichkeiten, aber von Jesus zugänglich gemacht: sein Kern ist die Selbsthingabe, die den Mensch dazu zwingt, auf seine eigene Natur zu verzichten, ihm aber eine Seligkeit gibt, die der Schöpfergott nie schenken könnte.

Wahrheit des Evangeliums gegangen seien (*Nam et ipsum Petrum ceterosque, columnas apostolatus, a Paulo reprehensos opponunt, quod non recto pede incederent ad evangelii ueritatem*)" (Übersetzung Karl Adam/Heinrich Kellner, *Tertullians sämtliche Schriften* II [Köln: DuMont-Schauberg, 1882] von mir korrigiert). Vgl. Norelli, „La funzione" (s. oben Anm. 20). Dazu Tertullian, *De Praescriptione* 33.
23 Enrico Norelli, „Marcion et les disciples de Jésus," *Apocrypha* 19 (2008): 9–42 [erschienen März 2010].
24 S. oben Anm. 11.

6 Paulus und sein Evangelium als der einzige Weg zu Jesus und seinem Vater

Selbstverständlich nahm Markion in der Kirche seiner Zeit sowie in der Überlieferung über Jesus und die Anfänge des christlichen Glaubens ein ganz anderes Verständnis des Evangeliums wahr, das die Kontinuität mit der Religion Israels betonte und die Beachtung zumindest der ethischen Vorschriften des Gesetzes, vor allem der Zehn Gebote, positiv bewertete. Er war aber davon überzeugt, dass eine solche Einstellung das Evangelium zerstöre und dass kein Evangelium mehr dort existiere, wo sie sich durchgesetzt hatte. Was aber konnte dann die Übereinstimmung der gegenwärtigen Verkündigung mit der Botschaft Jesu garantieren? Der scheinbar einfachsten Lösung, d. h. dem Vertrauen auf die fehlerfreie Übermittlung jener Botschaft durch Jesu Jünger, hatte Markion sich verschlossen. Die kirchliche Institution als solche war aus seiner Sicht durch die Verwirrung von Evangelium und Gesetz, von gutem und gerechtem Gott disqualifiziert worden; der Inhalt der Tradition, sowohl der mündlichen wie auch der schriftlichen, war von derselben Kontamination verzerrt worden. Sowohl die Institution wie auch die Überlieferung sind Markion daher ganz wertlos geworden. Der einzige Faden, der die gegenwärtigen Gläubigen mit der echten Verkündigung Jesu verbinden kann, läuft über Paulus. Markion hat aber eine mündliche Tradition oder eine Personenfolge, auf die die Lehre des Paulus sich stützen konnte, nicht gefunden bzw. nicht finden wollen.[25] Er war davon überzeugt, dass diese Lehre nur noch in den zehn Paulusbriefen und in dem Evangelium, das er mit Paulus verband, vorhanden sei: diese begrenzte Schriftensammlung erhielt daher eine entscheidende Bedeutung als der einzige Ort, an dem man dem Evangelium Jesu noch begegnen kann.

Hier wird die normative Autorität zum ersten Mal – soweit wir wissen – nicht dem Inhalt einer vom Vorrang ihrer Träger garantierten Überlieferung zugeschrieben, sondern nur einer Sammlung bestimmter schriftlicher Texte, und zwar

---

[25] Die Frage nach der Überlieferung der Botschaft des Paulus wurde in den alten lateinischen Prologen zu den Paulusbriefen gestellt, aber nur für die Zeit von der Gründung der jeweiligen Gemeinden bis zur Abfassung der Briefe. Trotz der Meinung der meisten Forscher bin ich überzeugt, dass diese Prologe wirklich markionitisch (obwohl nicht von Markion selbst verfasst, sondern später) sind, wie es Harnack – allerdings mit unzureichender Begründung – richtig gesehen hatte: vgl. meinen Nachweis in Enrico Norelli, „La tradizione ecclesiastica negli antichi prologhi latini alle epistole paoline", in *La tradizione: forme e modi. XVIII Incontro di studiosi dell'antichità cristiana, Roma 7-9 maggio 1989*, Studia ephemeridis „Augustinianum" 31 (Rom: Institutum Patristicum „Augustinianum", 1990): 301–324.

wegen der solchen Texten eigenen Fähigkeit, unabhängig von der Eigenschaft ihrer Tradenten durch die Zeit verhältnismäßig intakt zu bleiben. Falls ein schriftlicher Text geändert oder gar entstellt worden ist, besteht prinzipiell die Möglichkeit, die ursprüngliche Gestalt durch eine in einem gewissen Sinne philologische Arbeit wiederzufinden. Wo man sich dagegen im Wesentlichen auf eine mündliche Überlieferung stützt, hat die Wiedererlangung einer ursprünglichen Gestalt der Botschaft keinen eigentlichen Sinn und ist eine saubere Trennung echter und gefälschter bzw. späterer Elemente unmöglich. Nur die Schrift erlaubte Markion so vorzugehen, wie er es für angemessen hielt: er behielt den herkömmlichen Text so getreu wie möglich bei, hier und dort etwas streichend, manchmal nur ein Wort oder einen Teil eines Wortes ändernd; soweit er konnte, gewann er nur durch Auslegung den für ihn richtigen Sinn.

7 Ein Vergleich: Papias von Hierapolis und der Vorrang der mündlichen Überlieferung

Ein Vergleich mit einer anderen Lösung des Problems des Zugangs zur echten Verkündigung Jesu kann hier hilfreich sein. Nicht lange Zeit vor Markion (wahrscheinlich um 120) verfasste Papias, Bischof der christlichen Gemeinde von Hierapolis in Phrygien, sein Werk *Erklärungen der Orakel*[26] *des Herrn* in fünf Büchern, von dem nur wenige Fragmente erhalten sind. Eins von diesen ist ein Auszug aus dem Vorwort, den der Kirchenhistoriker Eusebius von Cäsarea in seiner *Kirchengeschichte* anführt (3,39,3–4):

> 3. Ich zögere aber nicht, für dich auch das, was ich von den Presbytern genau erfahren und genau im Gedächtnis behalten habe,[27] mit den Erklärungen zu verbinden, mich verbürgend für dessen Wahrheit. Denn nicht hatte ich, wie die meisten, Freude an denen, die vieles reden, sondern an denen, welche das lehren, was wahr ist; auch nicht an denen, die die fremdartigen Gebote im Gedächtnis haben, sondern an denen, die die vom Herrn dem Glauben gegebenen und von der Wahrheit selbst kommenden (Gebote im Gedächtnis haben).
>
> 4. Wenn aber irgendwo jemand, der den Presbytern nachgefolgt war, kam, erkundigte ich mich nach den Berichten der Presbyter: Was hat Andreas oder was hat Petrus gesagt, oder

---

26 Das griechische Wort *logia*, das Papias hier benutzt (die Überschrift des Werkes liefert Eusebius von Cäsarea, *Kirchengeschichte* 3,39,1), meint üblicherweise „Orakel"; in einem Papiasfragment (*Kirchengeschichte* 3,39,15–16) betrifft es offenbar die Taten und Worte Jesu und es ist wahrscheinlich, dass es im Titel des Papias diesen Sinn hatte.
27 Andere mögliche, vermutlich bessere Übersetzung von *mnêmoneuô*: „genau redigiert habe".

was Philippus oder was Thomas oder Jakobus oder was Johannes oder was Matthäus oder irgendein anderer der Jünger des Herrn, was ja auch Aristion und der Presbyter Johannes, (beide) des Herrn Jünger, sagen. Denn ich war der Ansicht, dass die aus Büchern (stammenden Berichte) mir nicht soviel nützen würden wie die (Berichte) von der lebendigen und bleibenden Stimme.

Papias behauptet hier, er habe seine Kenntnis der „vom Herrn dem Glauben gegebenen" Gebote durch eine mündliche Tradition erhalten, die auf die „Älteren", die *presbyteroi*, zurückgeht. In seiner Darstellung sind diese Leute etwa einer Generation von Tannaiten, d. h. von spezialisierten Überlieferern jüdischer Traditionen in den ersten zwei Jahrhunderten n. Chr. vergleichbar. Nach Papias hatten Jesu unmittelbare Jünger seine Lehre ihren eigenen Schülern übermittelt, d. h. den *presbyteroi*, die sie ihrerseits ihren Schülern weitergaben usw. Anders gesagt: die wahre Lehre wie auch die richtige Praxis gelangen zu ihren Empfängern durch eine persönliche Beziehung. Wenn Papias behauptet, dass er sich für die Wahrheit dessen, was er gelernt hat, verbürgen kann, so muss dies bedeuten, dass er sich für die Traditionskette der Lehrer verbürgen kann, was dem rabbinischen Modell entspricht.

In diesem Sinn können wir auch das Ende der zitierten Stelle verstehen: Warum sollte die lebende Stimme den Büchern überlegen sein und noch mehr, wie kann sie als „bleibend" gelten im Gegensatz zum geschriebenen Wort, das für unsere Empfindung viel feststehender und dauerhafter ist? Loveday Alexander hat die Behauptung des Papias mit einem antiken Topos verglichen: erstens wird eine Kunst oder Technik nicht so sehr durch Bücher gelernt, sondern viel eher durch die praktische Übung unter der Führung eines Meisters; zweitens ist eine mündliche rhetorische Leistung unvergleichlich wirksamer und deshalb notwendiger als ein schriftlicher Text; drittens lernt man viel besser aus der lebendigen Stimme des Lehrers als aus Büchern.[28] Die Formulierung des Papias ist sicher de-

---

[28] Loveday C.A. Alexander, „The Living Voice. Scepticism Towards the Written Word in Early Christian and Graeco-Roman Texts" in *The Bible in Three Dimensions*, hrsg. von David J.A. Clines/Stephen E. Fowl/Stanley E. Porter, JSOT Supplement 87 (Sheffield: JSOT Press, 1990): 221-247. Richard Bauckham, *Gesù e i testimoni oculari*, trad. Italiana (Chieti/Roma: Edizioni GBU, 2010): 29–42, folgt Alexander und erweitert die Anwendung des Prinzips auf die antike Geschichtsschreibung, denn er meint, dass das Werk des Papias diesem literarischen Genus angehört. Für eine kurze Auseinandersetzung mit Alexanders These darf ich auf Enrico Norelli, „La notion de ‚mémoire' nous aide-t-elle à mieux comprendre la formation du canon du Nouveau Testament?", in *Le canon des Écritures dans les traditions juive et chrétienne*, hrsg. von Philip S. Alexander/Jean-Daniel Kaestli, Publications de l'Institut romand des sciences bibliques 4 (Lausanne: Editions du Zèbre, 2007): 169–206, hier 190–192, verweisen.

nen verwandt, die innerhalb der antiken Literatur in solcher Kontexten verwendet werden, und es stimmt auch, dass die antike Geschichtsschreibung – wie Richard Bauckham betont hat – die mündliche Information begünstigt, die sowohl unmittelbar wie auch durch eine begrenzte Zahl von Zeugen weitergegeben worden sein kann.[29] Einige für die von Alexander und Bauckham erwähnten Bereiche wichtige Merkmale fehlen jedoch bei Papias: es handelt sich einerseits um das Motiv der Übung und der Nachahmung, andererseits um die bei den Historikern beliebte Idee, dass der Historiker seine Kenntnis unmittelbar von den Augenzeugen oder mindestens von einer möglichst kleinen Kette von Tradenten erhalten muss. Dies zeigt m. E., dass Papias den Topos zwar aufnimmt, ihn aber umgestaltet, damit dieser anderen, der Überlieferung der Taten und Worte Jesu eigenen Bedürfnissen entsprechen kann.

Was Papias mit seinen Ausführungen meint[30] ist m. E., dass das je vom Lehrer zum Schüler weitergegebene mündliche Wort eine Art stetigen Strom bildet. Noch wichtiger ist, dass dieses Wort durch die Kontrolle der Überlieferungskette überprüft werden kann, soweit man jedes Glied in der Kette nennen kann. Ein Buch geht im Gegensatz dazu als gesonderter Gegenstand herum: ist es anonym, so kann man es mit keinem zuverlässigen Überlieferungsträger verbinden; trägt es einen Autorennamen, so könnte es pseudepigraphisch sein. So ist es nicht „bleibend", denn es gehört nicht einem bleibenden und autorisierten Überlieferungsstrom an. Ein anderes Fragment aus dem Werk des Papias ist einschlägig: die wohlbekannte Darstellung der Abfassungsverhältnisse des Markusevangeliums (Eusebius, *Kirchengeschichte* 3,39,15) wird durch die Aussage „auch dies sagte der Presbyter" eingeleitet. Dies ist äußerst wichtig, denn es zeigt, dass das Markusevangelium nach Papias nur deshalb als zuverlässig gelten konnte, weil ein autorisierter Träger mündlicher Überlieferung (der Presbyter) für es bürgte; der Inhalt des Fragments zeigt, dass bestimmte Einwände gegen das Markusevangelium vorgebracht worden waren und dass die Erklärung des Presbyters sie zur Seite schieben sollte.

Papias kannte und benutzte also Bücher über Jesus (in seinen Fragmenten ist das Wort Evangelium nicht zu finden), er nennt ja die Werke des Markus und des Matthäus, solche Bücher sind aber für ihn nur in Beziehung zur mündlichen

---

29 Siehe auch Samuel Byrskog, *Story as History – History as Story. The Gospel Tradition in the Context of Ancient Oral History*, WUNT 123 (Tübingen: Mohr Siebeck, 2000) bes. 48–65.
30 Die Argumente für meine Papias-Interpretation finden sich ausführlich in Enrico Norelli, *Papia di Hierapolis: Esposizione degli oracoli del Signore. I frammenti. Introduzione, testo, traduzione e note*, Letture cristiane del primo millennio 36 (Milano: Paoline Editoriale libri, 2005).

Tradition annehmbar. Daneben kann er ohne Probleme auch Worte Jesu anführen, die nicht in den vier kanonisch gewordenen Evangelien stehen, so z. B. das Wort über die wunderbare Fruchtbarkeit der Erde im zukünftigen Reich Jesu (bei Irenäus von Lyon, *Gegen die Häresien* 5,33,3–4) oder „eine andere Geschichte über eine Frau, die wegen vieler Sünden vor dem Herrn angeklagt worden war; diese (Erzählung) enthält das Hebräerevangelium", (Eusebius, *Kirchengeschichte* 3,39,17); wir wissen übrigens nicht, ob Papias diese Geschichte dem Hebräerevangelium, einer anderen schriftlichen Quelle oder der mündlichen Überlieferung entnommen hat.[31] Mehrere Forscher haben in den letzten Jahren zu beweisen versucht, dass Papias die Sammlung der vier Evangelien schon kannte und als seine eigentliche normative Quelle benutzte. Ich meine dagegen nicht nur, dass diese These nicht nachweisbar ist, sondern vielmehr, dass eine derartige Position allem, was wir über Papias wissen können, widersprechen würde.[32] Solange er Überlieferung durch Leute empfängt, die er als zuverlässig betrachtet, gilt ihm diese Überlieferung als nicht weniger wichtig, ja wahrscheinlich als noch wichtiger als schriftliche Texte, die dieselben oder ähnliche Traditionen enthalten.

8 Der Vorrang der Schrift bei Markion

Nun war dies der Fall, weil Papias der kirchlichen Überlieferung vertraute, soweit sie durch eine Folge von Lehrern und Schülern garantiert wurde, die als vertrauenswürdig angesehen werden konnte. Markion hatte dagegen, wie wir gesehen haben, alles Vertrauen zu jeder Form kirchlicher Überlieferung verloren. Diese Überzeugung führte ihn zu einer umgekehrten Interpretation der christlichen Anfänge und der Weise, wie die Lehre Jesu weitergegeben worden war. Er konnte daher keinen positiven Gebrauch von der Überlieferung mehr machen. Er musste sich auf etwas stützen, das in irgendeiner Weise von jener Überlieferung unabhängig sein konnte, d. h. gerade auf jene Schriften, die Papias als nur begrenzt nützlich betrachtete, weil sie außerhalb des Traditionsstromes zirkulierten und es nötig hatten, durch ein Eintreten der mündlichen Tradition für sie zu einem bestimmten Punkt derselben Tradition, d. h. der „bleibenden Stimme", fixiert zu

---

31 Norelli, *Papia di Hierapolis* (s. oben Anm. 30), 331–335.
32 Enrico Norelli, „Papias de Hiérapolis a-t-il utilisé un recueil ‚canonique' des quatre évangiles?", in *Le canon du Nouveau Testament. Regards nouveaux sur l'histoire de sa formation*, hrsg. von Gabriella Aragione/Eric Junod/Enrico Norelli, Le monde de la Bible 54 (Genève: Labor et Fides, 2005): 35–85.

werden. Gerade das, was die Schriften für Papias „schwach" machte, machte sie „stark" für Markion: die Tatsache, dass sie von der „Tradition" getrennt werden konnten. Als die Tradition in Markions Augen zusammenbrach, fand er in den Schriften die einzig mögliche Stütze. Nicht in irgendwelchen Schriften selbstverständlich, sondern in solchen, die vom einzigen christlichen Missionar stammten, der nach Markion das Evangelium richtig verstanden und verkündigt hatte. Nach der Zeit des Paulus war die Kirche von der entstellten Überlieferung überflutet worden, seine Briefe und das seine Botschaft enthaltende Evangelium waren aber verfügbar geblieben und brauchten nur von späteren Verzerrungen befreit und richtig ausgelegt zu werden. Markion widmete sich daher der Wiederherstellung des Urtextes durch rationales Vorgehen.

Christoph Markschies hat neuestens „das primär philologische Interesse Marcions" nochmals betont und mit Recht an die Beobachtungen Harnacks und von Campenhausens erinnert, nach denen die Schüler Markions die Sammlung des letzteren nicht als „kanonisch" betrachteten und den von ihrem Meister etablierten Text immer wieder änderten.[33] Man könnte immerhin fragen, ob man aus dieser an sich richtigen Erkenntnis ohne weiteres folgern darf, „dass Marcion offensichtlich auch nicht intendierte, einen neuen ‚Kanon' heiliger Schriften vorzulegen, sondern die philologisch korrekte Edition eines gründlich korrumpierten Textes erstellen wollte. [...] er intendierte nicht, einen ‚Kanon' zu schaffen, sondern korrigierte einen Text eines bereits bestehenden ‚Kanons'."[34] Dass Markion einen seiner Ansicht nach korrumpierten Text verbessern wollte, steht außer Zweifel, wie auch, dass der von ihm korrigierte Text von ihm selbst und von seinen Schülern nicht als unantastbar und in diesem Sinn nicht als ‚kanonisch' angesehen wurde. Aber wie kann man daraus den Schluss ziehen, dass die Sammlung, deren Text Markion philologisch korrigieren wollte, „ein bereits bestehender ‚Kanon'" war? Und welche Quelle berechtigt uns zu denken, dass die Sammlung „(Lukas-)Evangelium + (10) Paulusbriefe" schon irgendwo im Christentum einen „Kanon" bildete? Was Markschies schon für Papias, d. h. für die Zeit vor Markion, mit Charles E. Hill als „kanonisch" anzunehmen scheint, ist eventuell die Vier-Evangelien-Sammlung.[35] Hills Stellung zu dieser Frage billige

---

33 Markschies, *Kaiserzeitliche christliche Theologie* (s. oben Anm. 3), 245–261, bes. 254 (daher das Zitat) und 258–259. Über Markion als Philologe siehe auch Robert M. Grant, „Marcion and the Critical Method", in *From Jesus to Paul. Studies in Honour of Francis Wright Bear*, hrsg. von Peter Richardson und John C. Hurd (Waterloo: W. Laurier, 1984): 207–215.
34 Markschies, *Kaiserzeitliche christliche Theologie* (s. oben Anm. 3), 259.
35 Markschies, *Kaiserzeitliche christliche Theologie* (s. oben Anm. 3), 250–251.

ich nicht,³⁶ aber auch wenn man sie teilt, spricht sie für einen Vier-Evangelien-Kanon und nicht für einen Nur-Lukas-Kanon.³⁷ Meiner Meinung nach sollte man lieber sagen, dass weder Markions korrigierter Text noch seine Sammlung als solche von ihm bzw. von seinen Anhängern als unantastbar betrachtet wurden (denn, wie gesagt, die Pastoralbriefe wurden von späteren Markioniten benutzt); dies zwingt aber keinesfalls dazu anzunehmen, dass die Schriftensammlung, die Markion als Grundlage seiner Ansichten heranzog, schon vor ihm irgendwie „kanonisiert" worden war. Ich würde eher vorschlagen, dass sowohl die Grenzen der Sammlung wie auch ihre textliche Gestalt der inneren Logik des Systems Markions gehorchten, was ich auf den nächsten, letzten Seiten zu begründen versuche.

9 Hat Markion den Kanon des Neuen Testaments gestiftet?

Die Forscher haben lange darüber diskutiert, ob Markion als der echte Stifter des neutestamentlichen Kanons anzusehen ist; dies war z. B. die Meinung von zwei großen Historikern der Alten Kirche im 20. Jahrhundert, Adolf von Harnack³⁸ und Hans von Campenhausen.³⁹ Es ist wahr, dass wir vor Markion keine Behauptung

---

36 Vgl. meine Auseinandersetzung mit seinem Beitrag in Norelli, *Papia di Hierapolis* (s. oben Anm. 30), 505–521.
37 Natürlich könnte man jederzeit behaupten, dass die Ausschaltung des Matthäus-, Markus- und Johannesevangeliums einen Teil von Markions philologischem Unternehmen darstellte!
38 Vgl. z.B. Harnack, *Marcion* (s. oben Anm. 10), 71–72: „die Tatkraft M.s liegt hier darin, dass er nicht einige christliche Texte verbessern, **sondern dass er der Gemeinde Christi eine neue Bibel schaffen wollte**. Das Evangelium des Lukas und die Paulusbriefe hat er bearbeitet, **um sie zusammenzustellen und dieses Corpus an die Stelle des AT zu setzen**. Sowohl die Zusammenstellung im Sinne eines einheitlichen Kanons als die Idee, das AT durch eine neue Sammlung abzulösen, sind sein Werk, und dieses Werk hat er der grossen Kirche siegreich aufgenötigt" (von Harnack gesperrt); ebenda 442*–444*; s. auch Adolf von Harnack, *Lehrbuch der Dogmengeschichte. Erster Band: Die Entstehung des kirchlichen Dogmas*, 5. Auflage (Tübingen: J.C.B. Mohr (Paul Siebeck), 1931), 306, und schon ders., *Die Entstehung des Neuen Testaments und die wichtigsten Folgen der neuen Schöpfung*, Beiträge zur Einleitung in das Neue Testament 6 (Leipzig: J.C. Hinrichs, 1914).
39 Hans Freiherr von Campenhausen, *Die Entstehung der christlichen Bibel*, Beiträge zur historischen Theologie 39 (Tübingen: J.C.B. Mohr (Paul Siebeck), 1968), 174–194; vgl. 174: „Idee und Wirklichkeit einer christlichen Bibel sind von Markion geschaffen worden, und die Kirche, die

der Notwendigkeit einer Schriftensammlung als einzig normative Quelle der christlichen Lehre kennen. Er ist der Erste, für den nunmehr das richtige Verständnis des Gebots Jesu nur über das geschriebene Wort möglich ist und bleiben wird.[40] Ich möchte dazu noch drei Bemerkungen anfügen.

Erstens war der wahre „Kanon" Markions sein hermeneutischer Grundsatz eines radikalen Gegensatzes zwischen Gesetz und Evangelium, der sich seinerseits auf die Erkenntnis stützte, dass das Evangelium Jesu die absolute, den Menschen als solchen überhaupt verborgene und in diesem Sinn wirklich transzendente Güte Gottes offenbarte. Zwischen diesem Grundsatz und der Schriftensammlung besteht übrigens eine Art Zirkel, denn die Grundüberzeugung Markions begründet die Auswahl gerade jener Schriften und wird zugleich von deren Inhalt begründet.

Zweitens ist es nicht ganz richtig, von einem Kanon Markions zu sprechen, wenn dieses Wort ein textliches Ganzes bedeuten soll, das nicht mehr geändert werden darf – zumindest prinzipiell, denn die Textvarianten in den Handschriften und Zitaten der kanonisch gewordenen Schriften beweisen, dass solche Texte neuen theologischen Anschauungen des öfteren angepasst wurden. Wie erwähnt und wie Harnack längst erkannt hat, haben die Markioniten nach Markion den Text weiter „verbessert" und die Pastoralbriefe hinzugefügt, was zeigt, dass sie – wie ohne Zweifel auch Markion selbst – den von Markion korrigierten Text nicht als unantastbar betrachteten.

---

sein Werk verwarf, ist ihm hierin nicht vorangegangen, sondern – formal gesehen – seinem Vorbild nachgefolgt"; vgl. schon ders., „Marcion et les origines du canon néotestamentaire", *Revue d'histoire et de philosophie religieuses* 46 (1966): 213–226. Für eine informative und ausgewogene Bewertung der deutschen Kanonforschung in Deutschland s. Christoph Markschies, „Epoques de la recherche sur le canon du Nouveau Testament en Allemagne: quelques remarques provisoires", in *Le canon du Nouveau Testament*, hrsg. von Aragione/Junod/Norelli (s. oben Anm. 32), 11–34.

40 Moll, *The Arch-Heretic Marcion* (s. oben Anm. 10), 104, bemerkt, dass die Voraussetzung für die Bestimmung einer Schriftensammlung war, dass Markion sich als in einer Zeit lebend betrachtete, die später als und verschieden von der Zeit der Urgemeinde war. Es sei seine „Verschwörungstheorie" gewesen, die ihm erlaubte zu entdecken, dass es eine Zeit gegeben habe, in der das Evangelium und die Briefe verfasst wurden, dann eine andere, in der sie verfälscht wurden, endlich eine dritte und gegenwärtige, in der ihre echte Gestalt wiedererlangt wird. Markion habe empfunden, dass dies die Zeit war, in der die Heilige Schrift nicht mehr hergestellt, sondern nur noch ausgelegt werden konnte. Diese der Ansicht Bartons (s. unten) entgegengesetzte Meinung scheint mir zu schematisch zu sein.

Einige Bemerkungen über bestimmte Thesen John Bartons sind wahrscheinlich an dieser Stelle angebracht.[41] Barton behauptet, Markion habe die jüdischen Heiligen Schriften als für Christen unbrauchbar verworfen, insoweit sie einen Gott vorstellten, der verschieden vom Vater Jesu war; Markion habe jedoch nicht beabsichtigt, sie durch eine christliche Heilige Schrift zu ersetzen. Was er unternahm, sei dasselbe, was mehrere christliche Autoren vor und neben ihm versuchten, nämlich eine schriftliche Sammlung der verfügbaren Überlieferungen über Jesus unter Ausscheidung von Inkonsequenzen und Widersprüchen herzustellen. Markion habe genau das getan, was sein bevorzugter Evangelist, Lukas, sich als Ziel gesetzt hatte: eine bessere Fassung von Jesu Taten und Worten aufzuschreiben, als es seine Vorgänger vermocht hatten. Markion habe aber nicht gesehen, dass er damit zu spät kam, weil der Zeitraum schon zu Ende war, in dem ein solches Unternehmen als möglich und wünschenswert angesehen wurde. Die Abfassung von weiteren Texten über Jesus mit einem harmonisierenden Ziel wurde nämlich durch die Annahme der festen Sammlung und des festen Textes der vier Evangelien mehr und mehr ersetzt, wobei Widersprüche nunmehr dadurch beseitigt wurden, dass man zeigte, dass sie nur scheinbare waren. Deshalb kann Barton schreiben: „Marcion was, in effect, an evangelist, who unfortunately for him lived too late for this to be an acceptable profession."[42] Nun erscheint mir Bartons Behauptung als problematisch, dass Markion „a (very restricted) selection from the corpus of texts" herstellte, „which already existed and which must already have been recognized as sacred by many in the church – otherwise he would not have needed to insist on abolishing them."[43] Nun kannte Markion sicherlich mehr Schriften über Jesus als die, die er akzeptierte, aber woher wissen wir, dass er so sehr darauf beharrte, sie auszuscheiden? Noch wichtiger: wie kann Barton behaupten, dass viele Christen solche Texte als heilig erkannten,[44] und sich danach über einige Seiten (345–347) zu beweisen bemühen, dass „the Christian books were merely memory-joggers, non independently existing scriptural oracles. Christians knew about Jesus from the tradition, not essentially from books. Even though in practice it might be from a book that a given

---

41 Ich verweise hier nur auf John Barton, „Marcion Revisited", in *The Canon Debate*, hrsg. von Lee Martin McDonald und James A. Sanders (Peabody (MA): Hendrickson, 2002): 341–354, das in der Tat eine Synthese davon darstellt, was Barton in früheren Beiträgen entwickelt hat.
42 Barton, „Marcion Revisited" (s. oben Anm. 41), 348.
43 Barton, „Marcion Revisited"(s. oben Anm. 41), 342–343.
44 Dass er hier christliche Texte meint, zeigt seine Behauptung, dass „they *must already* have been recognized as sacred by *many* in the church" (Kursivierung von mir).

Christian learned something about Jesus, it was not a book considered as ‚scripture', a kind of Torah, but a book considered as a historical record?"[45] Mit der zweiten Ansicht würde ich (mit einigen Klarstellungen) übereinstimmen, dann aber darf die erste nicht angenommen werden und daher auch nicht die Auffassung, dass Markion darauf beharrt habe, dass die meisten von vielen als heilig anerkannten Texte beseitigt werden müssten.

Mein Haupteinwand ist folgender: Ich betrachte es als höchst unwahrscheinlich, dass Markion nur beabsichtigte, eine neue und bessere Fassung der Jesusüberlieferung zu schaffen, wobei die schriftliche Fassung keine wesentlichen Unterschiede im Vergleich mit der mündlichen Überlieferung aufwies. Warum hätte er dann dem Evangelium eine Sammlung von zehn Paulusbriefen hinzugefügt? Er hätte diesen Briefen höchstens einigen (sehr begrenzten) Stoff über Jesus entnehmen können, den er in seinem Evangelium hätte benutzen können. Die Tatsache, dass er das *corpus paulinum* bewahrte und sorgfältig korrigierte, beweist, dass er die Wichtigkeit geschriebener Dokumente (wie es Briefe notwendigerweise sind) betonte, in denen er die wahrheitsgetreue Gestalt des Evangeliums (d. h. der von Jesus kommenden und Jesus betreffenden Botschaft) finden konnte. Gerade weil – wie erwähnt – Markion glaubte, dass die gesamte umlaufende, sowohl mündliche wie schriftliche, Jesusüberlieferung wegen der Verwechslung zwischen dem Gott Israels und dem Gott Jesu völlig korrumpiert war, konnte er *nicht*, um die echte Gestalt der Lehre Jesu wiederzufinden, aus dem Ganzen der existierenden Traditionen einige Elemente seiner Vorlieben gemäß wählen: er *musste* Zeugnisse vorstellen, die nachweisbar auf Jesus selbst zurückgingen. Angesichts der damaligen Lage des Christentums, so wie er sie beurteilte, war dies nur über ein bzw. mehrere geschriebene Dokumente möglich, die von irgendeinem Autor stammten, der Offenbarung unmittelbar von Jesus empfangen hatte. Dies erklärt, dass die Paulusbriefe ihm so wichtig waren. Als er aber Auskunft über Jesu Tätigkeit und Lehre brauchte, musste er ein Evangelium aufnehmen: seine Wahl wurde dadurch gerechtfertigt, dass Paulus, als er „mein Evangelium" in seinen Briefen schrieb, einen existierenden schriftlichen Text meinte, der von Markion – wir wissen leider nicht, aus welchen Gründen – mit dem Lukasevangelium gleichgesetzt wurde.

Was an Bartons Argumentation aber richtig ist, ist die Beobachtung, dass Markion keinen unantastbaren Textkomplex liefern wollte, daher keinen Kanon im engeren Sinne. Dies bestätigt die Annahme, dass nicht eine Textsammlung,

---

45 Barton, „Marcion Revisited" (s. oben Anm. 41), 345.

sondern ein theologischer Grundsatz in seinen Augen der eigentliche Kanon, d. h. die wahre Norm war.

Drittens sollte man betonen, dass die besondere Art und die Existenzberechtigung der Schriftensammlung Markions von der Beziehung zwischen einer normativen Schriftensammlung auf der einen Seite und der Tradition auf der anderen Seite abhing. Markions Sammlung hatte offenbar zum Ziel, ohne Tradition auszukommen. Die späteren Markioniten beschränkten sich nicht darauf, die Sammlung einfach weiterzugeben: wie wir sahen, haben sie den Text weiter verbessert und die Pastoralbriefe sehr wahrscheinlich dem *Instrumentum* noch hinzugefügt. Wenn der lateinisch erhaltene *Laodicenerbrief* ein markionitisches Werk ist, wie Harnack annahm und wie es m. E. sehr wahrscheinlich ist (siehe oben), muss man ja annehmen, dass Markioniten einen Paulusbrief geschaffen haben, was Markion selbst doch wahrscheinlich nicht getan hätte.[46] Und wenn die auch lateinisch erhaltenen kurzen Prologe zu den Paulusbriefen einen markionitischen Ursprung haben, was ich ebenfalls – wie gesagt – für wahrscheinlich halte, hatten die Markioniten ihre eigenen Anschauungen über die Rezeptions- und Vermittlungsprozesse der paulinischen Verkündigung in den verschiedenen Gemeinden, die die Paulusbriefe empfangen hatten. Aber darauf ist zu achten: Nur die Empfänger der Briefe kommen für solche Rezeptions- und Traditionsprozesse in Betracht. Anders gesagt, konnte eine positiv bewertete „Tradition" für die Markioniten nur als eine aktive Rezeption der Briefe vorstellbar sein. Der orthodoxe Kanon war im Gegensatz dazu nicht nur mit der Vorstellung einer breiten kirchlichen Tradition vereinbar; er war insofern ein Ausdruck und ein Zeugnis jener Tradition, als er von verschiedenen Vertretern der apostolischen Generation angeblich verfasste Schriften enthielt.

---

46 Das sogenannte *Fragment von Muratori*, wohl etwa 200 n. Chr. entstanden, schreibt den Markioniten sogar zwei falsche Paulusbriefe zu: *fertur etiam ad laudecenses alia ad alexandrinos pauli nomine fincte ad heresem marcionis* (Zeile 63–65). Ein Alexandrinerbrief ist bislang nicht wiedergefunden worden; es ist schwierig, einem Vorschlag von Theodor Zahn zuzustimmen, der diesen Brief mit einer liturgischen Lesung (Epistel) identifizieren wollte, die sich im *Sacramentarium et Lectionarium Bobiense*, einer Handschrift aus dem 7. Jahrhundert (Paris. Lat. 13246) findet und die den Titel *Epistula Pauli apostoli ad Colossenses* trägt, mit dem Kolosserbrief jedoch nichts zu tun hat; s. Theodor Zahn, *Geschichte des neutestamentlichen Kanons. Zweiter Band: Urkunden und Belege zum ersten und dritten Band* (Erlangen und Leipzig: A. Deichert, 1890), 586–592.

10 Sollte die Frage „Markion und der Kanon" anders gestellt werden?

Die Frage „War Markion der Schöpfer des neutestamentlichen Kanons?" sollte daher besser wie folgt umformuliert werden: „Welche Rolle spielt eine Sammlung normativer schriftlicher Texte im System Markions einerseits und andererseits in einem System, das sich selbst als orthodox bezeichnete?". Das letztere kann ich an dieser Stelle nicht skizzieren, es liegt aber auf der Hand, dass beide Systeme voneinander höchst verschieden sind. Man muss allerdings zugleich anmerken, dass sie etwas Gemeinsames haben: Markions negative Bewertung der kirchlichen Tradition erlaubte ihm, früher zu erkennen, was die sogenannten Rechtgläubigen erst später verstehen lernten: dass apostolische Schriften umso mehr notwendig wurden, je mehr sich die Kirche von der Zeit der ersten Zeugen entfernte. Auf die Idee einer Überlieferung, die auch die apostolischen Schriften trägt, wurde natürlich nicht verzichtet, diese Idee wurde aber entscheidend umgestaltet, und zwar besonders in der Theologie des Irenäus, Bischof von Lyon in den achtziger und neunziger Jahren des 2. Jahrhunderts.[47]

Dies erlaubte der sogenannten Großkirche, ein Verständnis der christlichen Identität zu entwickeln, das die jüdische Bibel integrierte und das Christentum als die Verwirklichung des Plans Gottes mit Israel betrachtete. Eine Folge dieser Anschauung war, dass die Existenz Israels in der christlichen Zeit eine Abnormität darstellte und nur als negatives Beispiel und Zeugnis der Rebellion gegen den Willen Gottes betrachtet werden konnte. Wenn Markion gewonnen hätte – dies kann selbstverständlich nichts anderes als eine reine Hypothese sein – hätte das Judentum das Recht gehabt, seinen Platz in der Welt zu behalten, insofern es die effektive Verwirklichung des Willens eines Gottes war, und zwar des Gottes, der unsere Welt geschaffen hat. Natürlich hätten die Markioniten es als beschränkte und unzureichende Religion abgestempelt, sie hätten aber niemals angenommen, dass seine Existenz in der Welt nur einen Widersinn darstellen kann, denn es würde dem Willen des Gottes, der für die Welt verantwortlich ist, entsprechen.

---

47 Für die Lösung des Irenäus erlaube ich mir, auf Enrico Norelli, „Le statut des textes chrétiens de l'oralité à l'écriture et leur rapport avec l'institution au IIe siècle", in *Recueils normatifs et canons dans l'Antiquité. Perspectives nouvelles sur la formation des canons juif et chrétien dans leur contexte culturel. Actes du colloque organisé dans le cadre du programme plurifacultaire* La Bible à la croisée des savoirs *de l'Université de Genève, 11–12 avril 2002* hrsg. von Enrico Norelli, Publications de l'Institut romand des sciences bibliques 3 (Lausanne: Editions du Zèbre, 2004): 147–194 (hier 186–189) zu verweisen.

Sie hätten im Gegenteil behauptet, dass das Judentum in dieser Welt viel mehr am Platze ist als das Christentum, das die echte Abnormität in einer Welt darstellt, in der die selbstlose Liebe eigentlich unbegreiflich ist.[48]

---

[48] Aufgrund der langen Druckverzögerung konnten wichtige neuere Veröffentlichungen über Marcion nicht berücksichtigt werden; dazu vgl. besonders: Markus Vinzent, *Marcion and the Dating of the Synoptic Gospels*, Studia Patristica, Supplement 2 (Leuven; Paris; Walpole, MA, 2014); Dieter T. Roth, *The Text of Marcion's Gospel*, New Testament Tools, Studies and Documents 49 (Leiden; Boston, Brill, 2015); Matthias Klinghardt, *Das älteste Evangelium und die Entstehung der kanonischen Evangelien*, Band I: *Untersuchung*; Band II: *Rekonstruktion / Übersetzung / Varianten*, 2 Bände, TANZ 60/1-2 (Tübingen, Francke Verlag, 2015); Judith M. Lieu, *Marcion and the Making of a Heretic. God and Scripture in the Second Century* (Cambridge, Cambridge University Press, 2015). Diese Bücher bespreche ich in einem Aufsatz, der im Jahre 2017 erscheinen wird. Auch weitere Titel, die die hier erwähnten Themen betreffen, mussten außer Betracht bleiben, z.B. James D. G. Dunn, *Christianity in the Making 3: Neither Jew nor Greek. A Contested Identity* (Grand Rapids, Mich.; Cambridge, U.K., 2015) (vgl. hier, Fussnote 4).

Averil Cameron
Christian Literature and Christian History

The great scholar Hans Lietzmann, whose memory is honoured in this lecture, was a pioneer not only in the discipline of ecclesiastical history but also in that of early Christian literature. His *Kleine Texte*, editions of patristic texts for theological lecturers and students, show that he was interested in literary style, and in such literary topics as prose rhythm, early Christian poetry, and rhetoric. His remarks on Latinity in relation to Augustine indicate his respect for another great German scholar, Eduard Norden, whose *Antike Kunstprosa* was published in 1898; they also no doubt reflect his own classical training.[1] Lietzmann also revised the section on Christian literature by Paul Wendland for the third edition of Gercke and Norden's *Einleitung* in 1923. This included poetry as well as prose literature, and even if not complete, went as late as the sixth and seventh centuries, with mentions of Cyril of Scythopolis, John Moschus, Sophronius and Leontius of Neapolis. Lietzmann's publication on the *Vita* of Symeon the Stylite arose from his seminar at Jena in 1908. His work on *catenae* belongs to the early years of the twentieth century, when he was also interested in liturgical texts and in papyri.[2] The *Griechische christliche Schriftsteller* series originally focused on the first three centuries of Christianity, and Harnack's history of early Christian literature took the subject only up to Eusebius.[3] Lietzmann's scope was wider, as Christoph Markschies remarks in his introduction to the Hans-Lietzmann-Vorlesung of 2010

---

1 The notion of *Kunstprosa* in relation to Greek literature is also emphasized in Hans Lietzmann, „Das Problem der Spätantike," in *Sitzungsberichte der Preußischen Akademie der Wissenschaften* 31 (Berlin: Verlag der Akademie der Wissenschaften, 1927): 342–358.
2 On *catenae* as an "activité intellectuelle des lettrés" and a "kind of hermeneutics" in late antiquity see Mathilde Aussedat, "Une pratique érudite de lecture des textes bibliques: les chaînes exégétiques grecques," *Revue des études grecques* 121.2 (2008): 547–569; ead., "Les chaînes exégétiques: une forme littéraire et une pratique d'érudition florissantes dans le domaine de l'exégèse de la langue grecque," in *Le païen, le chrétien, le profane. Recherches sur l'Antiquité tardive*, eds. Benjamin Goldlust and François Ploton-Nicollet, with Sylvain J.-G. Sanchez (Paris: PUPS, 2009): 169–179.
3 Harnack's third unpublished part would have dealt with Christian writing in this period. On Harnack's privileging of the second and third centuries in Christian development, and his adoption of scientific terminology, see the useful discussion by Claudia Rapp, "Adolf Harnack and the palaeontological layer of church history," in *Ascetic Culture. Essays in Honor of Philip Rousseau*, eds. Blake Leyerle and Robin Darling Young (Notre Dame, Indiana: University of Notre Dame Press, 2013): 295–314; the GCS series as originally envisaged ended with Nicaea, but was extended to cover the first five centuries at the instigation of Wilamowitz.

by Martin Wallraff.[4] Lietzmann's *History of the Church* (volume 1 was published in 1932; Harnack had died in 1930) included, at least to some extent, the period we now think of as late antiquity. Unlike those of most scholars of today, Lietzmann's writings ranged over the New Testament period as well as the post-Constantinian era. But it is striking that he saw that what we might call Christian literary texts beyond the New Testament period were also part of the history of the church and of the development of early Christianity.

1 Introduction: Christian literature, patristics and late antiquity

Lietzmann was active at a time when the parameters of early Christian history and early Christian literature were still being established. We live now a century later than some of the publications I have mentioned. For much of that time the field of patristics has held sway. More recently, the concept and practice of patristics have been challenged by that of "late antiquity", especially as understood in the English-speaking world. I will not go here into the history of the concept of "late antiquity", which is certainly much older than its current understanding, and was recognised in German scholarship long ago. But in its current mode, late antiquity implies not only a longer chronological sweep but also an increasing inclusion of Christian writing in languages other than Greek – especially works written in Syriac, but also nowadays also works written in Arabic.[5] The field of late antiquity, unlike that of "patristics", is not generally concerned with theological questions, except in terms of their contribution to intellectual history, as

---

[4] Christoph Markschies, "Vorwort," in Martin Wallraff, *Kodex und Kanon. Das Buch im frühen Christentum* (Hans-Lietzmann-Vorlesungen 12; Berlin/Boston: De Gruyter, 2013): v–xv, at viii–x, setting out the history of the GCS series and announcing major funding for the continuation of this historic work.
[5] For the turn to the east, and the widening of scope to include the languages and cultures of the eastern Mediterranean, including the emergence of Islam see Averil Cameron, "Patristics and the emergence of Islam," in *Patristic Studies in the Twenty-first Century. Proceedings of an International Conference to Mark the 50th Anniversary of the International Association of Patristic Studies*, eds. Brouria Bitton-Askelony, Theodore de Bruyn, Carol Harrison and Oscar Velásquez (Turnhout: Brepols, in press); ead., ed., *Late Antiquity on the Eve of Islam* (Farnham: Ashgate, 2013), Introduction, xiii–xxxvii. Another current way of looking at this eastward turn is through the prism of "Abrahamic religions": see Guy G. Stroumsa, "Athens, Mecca, Jerusalem. The patristic crucible of the Abrahamic religions," *Studia Patristica* 62 (2013): 153–168.

I shall argue further below, and while Harnack had studied theology, his approach to the study of early Christianity and its texts was historical enough for him to be admitted to the Berlin Academy, from which theologians were traditionally excluded and for which he was supported by the Roman historian Theodor Mommsen.[6] In the case of Lietzmann, his membership of the Lutheran church was not an easy matter as he grew older, and became more and more concerned with the problems of church and state, in antiquity as well as in the Germany of his own day[7] – a matter which, as we will see, is not far below the surface in my lecture today, though in a very different way.

The place of theology, I would argue, is always uncertain in relation to ecclesiastical history, and still more so in relation to the field of late antiquity. Most of the scholars now engaged in writing about the literature of late antiquity are not themselves theologians, nor do they write from a confessional viewpoint. They may be interested in the history of doctrine in terms of the development and definition of orthodoxy and heresy (a major preoccupation in current scholarship), but they do not approach Christian texts from the primary point of view of the history of the church. Lietzmann could write on *Das Problem der Spätantike*, but naturally did not do so in the terms of today's scholarship. He interpreted late antique culture in terms of eastern influences, placing himself on the side of J. Strzygowski, and against the views of the art historian Alois Riegl, who is often now regarded as the initiator of the current conception of late antiquity (Lietzmann regarded his views as "quasi-Hegelian").[8] A recent discussion by a historian who himself wants to argue that late antiquity extended to the end of the

---

6 Rapp, "Adolf Harnack", 299.
7 Hans Lietzmann, *Das Problem Staat und Kirche im weströmischen Reich* (Abhandlungen der preußischen Akademie der Wissenschaften, philosophisch-historische Klasse 11; Berlin: De Gruyter, 1940), taking the reign of Constantine as its starting point.
8 Hans Lietzmann, *Das Problem der Spätantike*, 342–358. On Riegl (Alois Riegl, *Spätrömische Kunstindustrie* (Vienna: Österreichische Staatsdruckerei, 1901) see Lietzmann, *Das Problem der Spätantike*, 345; Orientalising: 353; the key elements Lietzmann takes to demonstrate this are late Greek literature (with Romanos as an example of the eastern influence, 349) and religion – that is, Christianity as an eastern religion. His remarks are made in the context of a framing discussion of the reliefs on the Arch of Constantine, taken by many, including Bernard Berenson, as the classic example of "decline" (for discussion see Jas Elsner, "From the culture of spolia to the cult of relics: The Arch of Constantine and the genesis of late antique forms," *Papers of the British School at Rome* 68 [2000]; 149–184). For Riegl as the originator of the modern positive interpretation of late antiquity: see Wolf Liebeschuetz, "The birth of late antiquity," *Antiquité tardive* 12 (2004): 253–261 with Jas Elsner, "The birth of late antiquity: Riegl and Strzygowski in 1901," *Art History* 55.3 (2002): 358–379; the classic work by Josef Strzygowski is *Orient oder Rom*.

millennium and included the early Islamic period in its eastward sweep maintains that Lietzmann "broadly followed Strzygowski in his positive evaluation of the Orient, yet saw Islam as a step too far".[9] This discussion, which surveys earlier ways of interpreting the period in the context of a powerful overarching argument that sees late antiquity as reaching its culmination with the emergence of Islam, reveals the strongly ideological overtones that have pervaded and still pervade scholarship on the crucial centuries when Christianity was becoming established. Yet it is important to recognize to the full the fact that "late antiquity" today is far from being defined merely in terms of Christianity, and certainly not in terms of the "triumph of Christianity". It can be seen, in contrast, as a period of intense religious ferment and debate, within which various forms of Christianity and heterodoxy cohabited with Judaism, forms of Neoplatonism, and later, with early Islam.[10] In such a context a linear model in terms of the history of the church no longer works, and of course still less a teleological narrative. At a recent conference in Jerusalem held to mark the fiftieth anniversary of the international patristic association (AEIP) the disciplinary boundaries of "patristics" were a recurring subject. A few years ago the North American Patristic Society (NAPS) debated whether to drop the term "patristics" from its name, but decided to keep it, and the Oxford Patristic Conference, which began in 1951, still retains the term. Yet it is important to note that both cover a great deal of scholarship on Christian literature that is neither traditionally "patristic" nor that falls within the traditional field of church history.

Despite this, only recently, at an event in Oxford at which she surveyed the history of *Studia Patristica*, the proceedings of the Oxford Patristic Conference, Professor Frances Young described its overall approach to texts as being that of

---

Beiträge zur spätantiken und frühchristlichen Kunst (Leipzig: J.C. Hinrichs, 1901), published in the same year as Riegl's book.
9 Garth Fowden, *Before and After Muhammad, The First Millenium Refocused* (Princeton: Princeton University Press, 2013), 39, following a lengthy discussion of Riegl and Strzygowski. A different view of the emergence of Islam can be found in Aziz al-Azmeh, *The Emergence of Islam in Late Antiquity. Allah and His People* (Cambridge: Cambridge University Press, 2014).
10 So Averil Cameron, *The Mediterranean World in Late Antiquity, c. 395–700*, 2nd rev. ed. (London: Routledge, 2012), 169–190. The "marketplace: idea of religious competition" is debated in David Engels and Peter Van Nuffelen, eds., *Religion and Competition in Antiquity* (Brussels: Éditions Latomus, 2014), and on the issues surrounding the much-discussed question of Christianization in the Roman empire see Averil Cameron, "Christian conversion in late antiquity – some issues," in *Conversion in Late Antiquity: Christianity, Islam and Beyond*, eds. Daniel Schwartz, Neil McLynn and Arietta Papaconstantinou (Oxford: Oxford University Press, in press).

philology and "historical criticism". She commented on the relative lack of hermeneutics and of post-modern criticism. On the same occasion Dr Mark Edwards mounted a defence of the view that patristics must still have the history of Christian dogma as its main concern. In general, though, while we still sometimes find the assumption that early Christian texts are valuable insofar as they are useful to the historian, a high percentage of recent contributions to *Studia Patristica* and other publications do approach them as pieces of writing, from the point of view of literary analysis. This suggests to me that there is a problem here that needs to be discussed.

With the "linguistic turn", and the wider move among scholars of late antiquity towards the analysis of discourse and rhetoric, the status of literature in early Christianity has risen to the fore. What kind of modern literary analysis can be applied?[11] How appropriate is such an analysis to Christian texts, and what is their relation to the history of Christianity?

In my book *Christianity and the Rhetoric of* Empire, published in 1991 but based on the Sather Lectures given at Berkeley in 1986, I argued that the rhetorical practices used in Christian writing after the New Testament period were themselves a factor in the process of Christianization, and, in turn, that Christian writers necessarily adopted rhetorical practices that allowed them to connect with the wider culture of the Roman empire. Christians could not and did not remain outsiders, either before or after the critical shifts in church and state relations in the reign of Constantine. The story can be, and naturally has been, written in terms of the history of power relations. Christian writing, Christian rhetorical practices and Christian modes of argumentation fulfilled clearly useful functions, for instance in arguing against pagans, Jews, heretics, or later, Muslims. Complex, learned and sophisticated methodologies were developed for use at church councils and in Scriptural exegesis. Christians had to be able to match their rivals on their own philosophical and rhetorical ground. Their scholarship and their deployment of texts had to be equal to theirs. A Christian knowledge economy had to be created.

Such a process has already been the subject of much recent scholarship, as has the status of early Christianity as a "book culture", and the place of books and book scholarship in the early Christian world – the use of books in early

---

11 The question is raised by Gilles Dorival, "Existe-t-il une recherche proprement littéraire dans le domaine de l'Antiquité tardive?," *TOPOI Orient-Occident* 4.2 (1994): 651–669.

Christianity is the subject of Martin Wallraff's contribution to the present series.¹² My question here is rather different, and I will not add to that debate. In contrast, my topic concerns what we might call the literary, rather than the intellectual, status of this deluge of written material by Christians in the Roman empire and late antiquity. Can it be regarded as "literature'" and if so, how should we approach it and with what conclusions?

There are of course many existing contributions on this topic, including histories of Christian literature as such.¹³ I am not concerned here, however, with patrologies, or similar handbooks, useful though they are.¹⁴ We need here to distinguish here between the broadly descriptive and the more analytic and theoretical. There is also a question of definition. Accordingly, I take "Christian literature" simply to refer to literary works written by Christians, without prejudging their intention or the extent of religious message. Alan Cameron's most recent book, *The Last Pagans of Rome* (2011), dealing with Latin literary culture in the

---

12 Wallraff, *Kodex und Kanon*; Anthony Grafton and Megan Hale Williams, *Christianity and the Transformation of the Book. Origen, Eusebius and the Library of Caesarea* (Cambridge, Massachusetts: Belknap Press of Harvard University Press, 2006); papers by Guy G. Stroumsa, including "The Scriptural movement of late antiquity and Christian monasticism," *Journal of Early Christian Studies* 16.1 (2008): 66–77, discussing also the concept of *Buchreligion* in Jan Assmann, *Die mosaische Unterscheidung, oder, Der Preis des Monotheismus* (Munich, Vienna: Carl Hanser Verlag, 2003): 145–151. Aspects of this "book culture" range from the concept of a canon, the use of and development of books as physical objects, and the move between, or relationship of, roll and codex, to the citation and exegesis of formative texts and the implications of "book religion" and "the Scriptural movement".
13 Notably Frances M. Young, Lewis Ayres, Andrew Louth, eds., *The Cambridge History of Early Christian Literature* (Cambridge: Cambridge University Press, 2004), covering the period from the New Testament to Cyril, with chapters on specific authors and types of writing, or social and historical context rather than on literary questions as such, though Frances Young's chapter (21) is directed at the use of classical genres by Christian authors in the fourth and fifth centuries. Part VI in Susan Ashbrook Harvey and David G. Hunter, eds., *The Oxford History of Early Christian Studies* (Oxford: Oxford University Press, 2008) is entitled "Expressions of Christian culture" and includes sections on literary forms such as apologetic, homiletic, hagiography and martyr acts, historiography, poetry and hymnography (Latin, Greek and Syriac) and philosophy, but not on literary issues as such.
14 For the latter, see for instance Claudio Moreschini and Enrico Norelli, *Storia della letteratura cristiana antica greca e latina*, 2 vols. (Brescia: Morcelliana, 1995–1996); Reinhart Herzog, *Spätantike. Studien zur römischen und lateinisch-christlichen Literatur* (Göttingen: Vandenhoeck & Ruprecht, 2002), and see Mark Vessey, "Literature, patristics, early Christian writing," in Ashbrook Harvey and Hunter, eds., *The Oxford Handbook of Early Christian Studies*, 43–65, at 51–58.

late fourth century,[15] has shown beyond question just how misleading it is to suppose that all literature written or sponsored by Christians necessarily had a religious purpose, or was aimed at attacking pagans; Christians could have literary aims themselves, and the term "Christian" then as now covered a huge variety of personal interpretations. But to put it very simply, does it follow that because a given writer identified himself or was identified by others, including modern critics, as "Christian", everything he wrote was written with a specifically Christian purpose?

The question obviously arises in particular ways in the case of historiography, and especially ecclesiastical history, not least because ecclesiastical historians in antiquity wrote explicitly with the intention of focusing on the history of the Christian church, and of explaining the place of Christianity in universal history. We are all familiar with the many different ways in which this scenario found expression in the genre. Yet historians of the church were also writing within a literary tradition, and used the techniques of rhetoric.[16] The ways in which these tensions played out inform one of the most active areas of current scholarship on late antique literature, and it seems increasingly artificial to separate ecclesiastical from secular or "classicizing" history-writing. But unless they are fully recognized and explored in each individual case the value of the work for the historian cannot be properly understood.

I believe that we may be at a turning point in relation to understanding early Christian literature. For reasons that I shall go on to explain, there is at this moment a veritable explosion of writing on the subject. Yet its starting points and its aims are equally uncertain. In this lecture I want to explore some of these issues and suggest some possible ways forward.

---

[15] See Mark Vessey, "The end of the pagan classics," *Journal of Roman Archaeology* 25 (2012): 939–947.

[16] Peter Van Nuffelen has recently made a forceful case for the need for rhetorical analysis in the case of Orosius's *Historiae adversus paganos*, of the early fifth century, a work commonly dismissed as derivative and superficial: Peter Van Nuffelen, *Orosius and the Rhetoric of History* (Oxford: Oxford University Press, 2012). Whereas the traditional approach to Orosius has been theological (Van Nuffelen, *Orosius*, 1–9, though contrasting this with the more historical approach of Adolf Lippold, *Rom und die Barbaren in der Beurteilung des Orosius*, Diss. Erlangen, 1952), Van Nuffelen offers a literary reading, against the earlier emphasis on content, on the grounds that "we need first to understand the form of the *Historiae* before we can grasp its content", ibid., 9. Van Nuffelen cites much recent relevant bibliography on these issues, including many works by German scholars, and see also Matthew S. Kempshall, *Rhetoric and the Writing of History 400–1500* (Manchester: Manchester University Press, 2011).

2 Christian writing in late antiquity – a "new intellectual history"?

Martin Wallraff's Lietzmann lecture of 2010, and other recent publications, have familiarized us with the idea of early Christianity as a book culture. Origen's library at Caesarea, and Eusebius's reading give us some idea. In the period from the fourth century onwards, the huge output of Christian writers is astonishing – treatises, commentaries, letters, exegesis. Some of this is accounted for by the need to preach and teach on a regular basis, and some also by the requirements of doctrinal argument against rivals, but the quantity far exceeds what was needed for either of these. It is also only partly explained by the challenge that was inherent in the development of Christianity as a Scriptural movement. The new position of the church after the reign of Constantine required from its leaders, who were mostly though not always bishops, a literary output in terms of justification, explanation, argument, and to some extent popularization. As time went on it also required formalized tools of argument in the shape of *florilegia* (collections of carefully chosen patristic and Scriptural extracts) and exegetical *catenae*. This was a vast intellectual enterprise, part of an attempt to formulate a Christian system of knowledge that would answer and replace existing theories, and eventually encompass everything.[17] Some modern scholars have referred to the study of this huge mass of writing as "a new intellectual history".[18] I shall have more to say on this way of looking at early Christian literature, but I will also argue that too much concentration on its function as promoting various forms of Christian orthodoxy and arguing out doctrinal issues leaves out something very important, namely the sheer stimulus, excitement and originality evident in the work of some Christian writers – in fact literature for its own sake. Is it possible to move from the idea that Christian literature is helpful insofar as it contributes to Christian history, the history of Christianity, to a consideration of early Christian literature as *literature*? In which case what critical parameters can be applied to it?

---

17 Hervé Inglebert, *Interpretatio Christiana. Les mutations des savoirs (cosmographie, géographie, ethnographie, histoire) dans l'Antiquité chrétienne, 30–600 après J.C.* (Paris: Institut d'études augustiniennes, 2001).
18 See Clark, *History, Theory, Text* (below, n. 20), 106–129, 159, with the review discussion of this book by Virginia Burrus, et al. in *Church History* 74 (2005): 812–836.

Many scholars have written about early Christian literature, including for example Frances Young in her book on the development of Christian Scriptural exegesis, where she discusses rhetorical strategies and writing techniques, but her Bampton Lectures, recently published, are more personal and also more theological – modern theology *through* or *with* the Fathers.[19] In contrast the American church historian Elizabeth Clark issued a rallying cry to other scholars when she argued that early Christian writing could not be exempt from the 'linguistic turn' that had had such a deep effect on other kinds of literary study. Her example met with a respectful reception, especially among North American scholars.[20] Another scholar who has been asking precisely my question about the literary status of early Christian writing for the past two decades is Mark Vessey, of the University of British Columbia in Canada.[21] Vessey in particular has stressed the problems that nowadays surround the very terms "Christianity" and "literature". Some scholars refer to "Christianities" in the plural so as to avoid essentialist assumptions; others advocate a much wider view of Christianity than merely doctrinal content – practice, liturgy, *habitus*, and indeed pluralism.[22] The two problems come together in that Christian literature cannot be separated from literature in general (or, to cite Vessey again, "literatures")[23]. Nor can it be separated from the idea of a "late antique culture", which assumes that writing about early Christian

---

19 Frances M. Young, *Biblical Exegesis and the Formation of Christian Culture* (Cambridge: Cambridge University Press, 1997); ead., *God's Presence. A Contemporary Recapitulation of Early Christianity* (Cambridge: Cambridge University Press, 2013).
20 Elizabeth A. Clark, *History, Theory, Text: Historians and the Linguistic Turn* (Cambridge, Massachusetts: Harvard University Press, 2004); ead., *Reading Renunciation: Asceticism and Scripture in Early Christianity* (Princeton: Princeton University Press, 1999). Clark surveys the field in "From patristics to early Christian studies," in Harvey and Hunter, eds., *The Oxford Handbook of Early Christian Studies*, 8–41, where she refers at 25–27 to "the new cultural theory"; see also Dale B. Martin and Patricia Cox Miller, eds., *The Cultural Turn in Late Ancient Studies. Gender, Asceticism and Historiography* (Durham, NC: Duke University Press, 2005), 1–21.
21 For instance Vessey, "Literature, patristics, early Christian writing", especially 49–51, with id., "The demise of the Christian writer and the remaking of 'late antiquity': from H.-I. Marrou's Saint Augustine (1938) to Peter Brown's holy man (1983)," *Journal of Early Christian Studies* 6.3 (1998): 377–381. I am grateful to Mark Vessey for sharing several papers with me and for engaging in stimulating discussion.
22 So Virginia Burrus, ed., *Late Ancient Christianity* (Minneapolis: Fortress, 2005); Derek Krueger, ed., *Byzantine Christianity* (Minneapolis: Fortress, 2006), both in the series People's History of Christianity. See also Éric Rebillard, *Transformations of Religious Practices in Late Antiquity* (Farnham: Ashgate, 2013). Problematics surrounding the concept of "literature": Mark Vessey, "Writing before literature: Derrida's Confessions and the Latin Christian world," in Miriam Leonard, ed., *Derrida and Antiquity* (Oxford: Oxford University Press, 2010): 289–320.
23 Vessey, "Literature, patristics, early Christian writing", 51–55.

literature is in fact an exercise in doing cultural history.[24] The explosion of late antiquity, to use the term made familiar in a critical article on the subject by the Italian scholar Andrea Giardina,[25] causes problems for existing disciplines, which have to give way or make room for it: for instance Byzantine studies and late Roman history, and importantly for us now, and especially in terms of works in Latin, the subject traditionally defined as the history of European literature.[26] But the postmodern anxieties around the term 'literature', as well as the broader understanding of Christianity within the spectrum of the study of religions also unsettle the traditional practice of patristics, and the equally traditional attachment to histories of Christian literature as contributing to the history of Christianity itself.

Finally, if early Christian literature needs to be re-inserted into the broad sweep of literature in general, one should expect in turn that critics of literature in the Roman empire should include Christian writing within their frame. This is by no means always the case at present. Christian writing is conspicuously absent from much of the large body of excellent recent scholarly work on the Second Sophistic, despite the obvious consideration that Christian writing and the Greek works of the Second Sophistic have in common many of the multiple issues surrounding the subject of Hellenism.[27] As we shall see below, a "Third Sophistic" has been proposed by some scholars dealing with late antique literary questions,

---

[24] So Clark, "From patristics to early Christian studies", 25–27; Vessey, "Literature, patristics, early Christian writing", 55–58; Martin and Cox Miller, eds., *The Cultural Turn*.
[25] Andrea Giardina, "Esplosione di tardoantico," *Studi Storici* 40 (1999): 157–180.
[26] On which see Vessey, "Literature, patristics, early Christian writing", 55–59.
[27] On which see Simon Swain, *Hellenism and Empire. Language, Classicism and Power in the Greek World, AD 50–250* (Oxford: Clarendon Press, 1996), with chapters on individual writers, none of them Christian; Swain hints at differences between the material he considers and Christian writing (122,131), including the Apocryphal Acts, but does not explain them (for the latter, which lend themselves to questions of narrative and fictionality, see Averil Cameron, *Christianity and the Rhetoric of Empire*, 89–119; Ronald F. Hock, J. Bradley Chance and Judith Perkins, eds., *Ancient Fiction and Early Christian Narrative* (Atlanta, Ga: Scholars Press, 1998)). In Simon Goldhill, ed., *Being Greek under Rome. Cultural Identity, the Second Sophistic and the Development of Empire* (Cambridge: Cambridge University Press, 2001), one of the chapters deals with Jewish material but none with Christian. It is worth noting that in 1892, as Claudia Rapp points out, Harnack had written the postscript to the German translation of Edwin Hatch's Hibbert Lectures on the theme *Griechentum und Christentum* (Rapp, "Adolf Harnack", 307). For "Hellenism" and early Christianity see recently Arnaud Perrot, ed., *Les chrétiens et l'hellénisme. Identités religieuses et culture grecque dans l'Antiquité tardive* (Paris: Éditions Rue d'Ulm, 2012); Christoph Markschies, *Hellenisierung des Christentums. Sinn und Unsinn einer historischen Deutungskategorie* (Forum Theologische Literaturzeitung 25; Leipzig: Evangelische Verlagsanstalt, 2012).

but the uncertain place of Christian authors within what has been proposed serves to underline their absence from the Second Sophistic that is the explicit model. There are indeed studies of the relation between the Second Sophistic and individual Christian writers, but we will look in vain for Christian literature in such central works on the latter as Tim Whitmarsh's *The Second Sophistic* or more recently his *Beyond the Second Sophistic. Adventures in Greek Postclassicism*, or in Thomas Schmitz's *Bildung und Macht*.[28] But if Christian literature is indeed open to literary approaches, it can hardly be separated off in this way. Such a compartmentalizing does no service either to Christian or to non-Christian works.

After this introduction, I want to go on to consider several current themes in the study of early Christian literature, focusing on the late antique period, and finally to make some suggestions for the future based on a particular example.

3 The instrumental approach

I will start with what seems to be the dominant approach in current scholarship, namely the assumption that early Christian literature was first and foremost *instrumental*: its aim was to win arguments and gain authority. Peter Brown's book, *Power and Persuasion in Late Antiquity* (1992), put the case very firmly, by arguing

---

[28] Tim Whitmarsh, *The Second Sophistic* (Oxford: Oxford University Press for the Classical Association, 1996), 9, claims that "Christianity can now be discussed as part of the same cultural and intellectual landscape as the pagan culture of the Roman east", but without doing so himself; in id., *Beyond the Second Sophistic. Adventures in Greek Postclassicism* (Berkeley: University of California Press, 2013), one chapter, again, deals with a subject from Hellenistic Judaism, but none with Christianity, though Whitmarsh himself observes the usual absence of both in standard accounts of postclassical Greek literature. See also id., *Greek Literature and the Roman Empire: The Politics of Imitation* (Oxford: Oxford University Press, 2001), and Thomas Schmitz, *Bildung und Macht: zur sozialen und politischen Funktion der zweiten Sophistik in der griechischen Welt der Kaiserzeit* (München: Verlag C.H. Beck, 1997). Nor does Christian material find a place in the otherwise very interesting collection by Jason König and Tim Whitmarsh, eds., *Ordering Knowledge in the Roman Empire* (Cambridge: Cambridge University Press, 2007). An exception is Jason König, *Saints and Symposiasts. The Literature of Food and the Symposium in Greco-Roman and Early Christian Culture* (Cambridge: Cambridge University Press, 2012), who admits some Christian works to the genre of "symposiastic literature" but see Averil Cameron, *Dialog und Debatte in der Spätantike* (Spielräume der Antike 3; Stuttgart: Franz Steiner Verlag, 2014; English version, *Dialoguing in Late Antiquity*, Hellenic Studies 65 [Washington, DC and Cambridge, Massachusetts: Center for Hellenic Studies, 2014]), Kap. 1; also unusual in including Christian material is Kendra Eshleman, *The Social World of Intellectuals in the Roman Empire: Sophists, Philosophers and Christians* (Cambridge: Cambridge University Press, 2012).

for the importance of *paideia* in the late antique Christian context. Unlike his earlier book about the rise of asceticism, *The Body and Society. Men, Women and Sexual Renunciation in Early Christianity* (1988), which does not foreground writing as a main element, or present its subject in theoretical terms, *Power and Persuasion* argues for *paideia* (demonstrated in eloquence) as a key element in the rise to power of Christian bishops and other leaders. *The Care of the Self*, volume 3 in Michel Foucault's *History of Sexuality* (1986) had very recently read Christian writing in terms of the history of power, and power has indeed been a major theme in many contributions on late antiquity since then.[29] In the last two decades we have also seen a huge emphasis on the themes of orthodoxy and heresy, suggesting that both, in their differing ways, were constructions of early Christian writing. Unlike the traditional concept of heresy as an aberration from the central Christian understanding of orthodoxy (admittedly a view sometimes still to be found), we know about most heresies from the writings of their opponents, who resorted to every possible technique of apologetic, polemic, rumour and innuendo.[30] Countless recent scholarly works expose the lengths to which some Christian writers would go, even the most respectable and even the most revered. Athanasius, for instance, is one of the worst offenders.[31] Eusebius, the foundational writer of ecclesiastical history, is recognized now as having presented a triumphalist narrative, making full use of rhetorical tropes and methods and aimed at persuasion.[32] Like any contemporary writer, he updated his work as the situation

---

29 For instance, Andrew Cain and Noel Lenski, eds., *The Power of Religion in Late Antiquity* (Farnham: Ashgate, 2009); the corollary of power is violence: Harold Drake, with Emily Albu, Susanna Elm, Michael Maas, Claudia Rapp, Michele Salzman, eds., *Violence in Late Antiquity. Perceptions and Practices* (Aldershot: Ashgate, 2006); Thomas Sizgorich, *Violence and Belief in Late Antiquity. Militant Devotion in Christianity and Islam* (Philadelphia: University of Pennsylvania Press, 2009).
30 For instance see Aline Pourkier, *L'hérésiologie chez Epiphane de Salamine* (Christianisme antique 4; Paris: Beauchesne, 1992); Averil Cameron, "How to read heresiology," in Martin and Cox Miller, eds., *The Cultural Turn in Late Ancient Studies*, 193–212; a special section in *JECS* edited by Virginia Burrus is devoted to the topic of heresy: *Journal of Early Christian Studies* 4.4 (1996): 403–513.
31 See David Gwynn, *The Eusebians: the Polemic of Athanasius of Alexandria and the Construction of the Arian Controversy* (Oxford: Oxford University Press, 2007). "Arianism" had already been deconstructed, for instance by Rowan Williams, *Arius: Heresy and Tradition* (London: Darton, Longman and Todd, 1987), and see id., ed., *The Making of Orthodoxy. Essays in Honour of Henry Chadwick* (Cambridge: Cambridge University Press, 1989).
32 A forceful view is put by Doron Mendels, *The Media Revolution of Early Christianity. An Essay on Eusebius's* Ecclesiastical History (Grand Rapids, Michigan: William B. Eerdmans pub., 1999).

changed, and in his other works he strengthened and amplified his main story. Even now the extent of his rewriting and adjustment in the *Vita Constantini* needs to be emphasized, together with his continuing commitment to the cause of publicity and persuasion, right up to the end of his life. We are better able to judge these issues of writing technique nowadays, and none of this should cause Eusebius to be dismissed as the dishonest historian seen by Jacob Burckhardt in the nineteenth century, though one of the many recent books on Constantine simply calls his picture wrong, with no further discussion.[33]

Examples of the instrumentalist interpretation of early Christian literature can easily be piled up. A case has been made for example for functionality in monastic literature and hagiography.[34] Exegesis, one of the key preoccupations of the period among Christian writers, was both useful and necessary. It made difficult passages in the Scriptures intelligible, but it also provided an armoury of explanations and parallels to be applied in doctrinal disputes. Christian exegesis of the Hebrew Scriptures goes back to the New Testament, and was essential if the Hebrew Scriptures were to be incorporated. It was also necessary in demonstrating the superiority of Christianity over Judaism, and a whole panoply of arguments was developed against real or supposed Jewish objections to Christian readings of the Scriptures. In the same way sets of argument, and modes of writing, existed in order to refute the heterodox – or indeed to create highly coloured pictures of supposed heretics. It is not surprising that words like "Medicine-chest", or "Armoury" were used to describe such works – remedies against dangerous opinions, or weapons to attack them. *Florilegia*, collections of citations, were just such collections of ready quotations on the basis of which a case could be made.

Recent re-evaluations of Eusebius include S. Inowlocki and Claudio Zamagni, eds., *Reconsidering Eusebius. Collected Papers on Literary, Theological and Theological Issues* (Leiden: Brill, 2011); Aaron P. Johnson, *Ethnicity and Argument in Eusebius's Praeparatio Evangelica* (Oxford: Oxford University Press, 2006); id., *Eusebius* (London: I.B. Tauris, 2013); Sébastien Morlet, "Écrire l'histoire selon Eusèbe de Césarée," *L'information littéraire* 57.3 (2005): 1–15; id., *La Démonstration évangélique d'Eusèbe de Césarée. Étude sur l'apologétique chrétienne à l'époque de Constantin* (Paris: Institut des études augustiniennes, 2009).

33 David Potter, *Constantine the Emperor* (Oxford: Oxford University Press, 2013), 303: "Clear and powerful in its message, *The Life of Constantine* is a deeply problematic book"…"The fundamental problem with Eusebius's history is that his picture of Constantine's struggle against paganism is wrong and that his understanding of Constantine's conversion is based on a fantasy".

34 Claudia Rapp, "The Literature of Early Monasticism: Purpose and Genre between Tradition and Innovation," in *Unclassical Traditions. Alternatives to the Classical Past in Late Antiquity*, eds. Richard Flower, Christopher Kelly, Michael Williams (Cambridge Classical Journal, Supplement; Cambridge: Cambridge University Press, 2010): 119–130.

Most scholars who have studied this huge quantity of Christian writing have assumed – and still assume – that it had a function, namely to promote this or that form of Christian doctrine, or in more contemporary terms to establish forms of Christian identity. The terms apologetic and polemic are constantly used,[35] though usually neither is clearly defined, and the latter is currently much overused. Nevertheless identity-formation has been and is one of the major themes in scholarship on early Christian texts from the second century onwards, and it is equally central to current approaches to late antique writing.[36] Several publications by the Finnish scholar Maijastina Kahlos, mainly about fourth-century material, and another recently edited by her, all argue in this direction.[37] They explore the language of polemic and exclusion, and with it the role of Christian writing in creating identity and at the same time identifying the "other" – the heretic, the pagan, the Jew. The language of polemic and heresiology is equally well studied in many late antique Christian works, including saints' lives, where it is often so embedded in the latter that it has simply been taken for granted. But this is also now well recognised. Hagiography, too, invariably had a purpose and

---

35 On the uncertainties of the term apologetic: Martin Goodman, Simon R.F. Price, Christopher Rowland and Mark J. Edwards, eds., *Apologetics in the Roman Empire* (Oxford: Oxford University Press, 1999).

36 Ethnicity, "identity" and "community" often go together, for instance in Stephen Mitchell and Geoffrey Greatrex, eds., *Ethnicity and Culture in Late Antiquity* (London and Swansea: Duckworth and the Classical Press of Wales; 2000), R.B. ter Haar Romeny, ed., *Religious Origins of Nations? The Christian Communities of the Middle East* (Leiden: Brill, 2010); Fergus Millar, *Religion, Language and Community in the Roman Near East: Constantine to Muhammad* (Oxford: Oxford University Press, 2013), as well as many other publications. A major strand in recent scholarship has been a focus on language-use in the eastern Mediterranean in late antiquity as a marker of culture and identity among eastern Christians and others: cf. Arietta Papaconstantinou, ed., *The Multilingual Experience in Egypt from the Ptolemies to the Abbasids* (Farnham: Ashgate, 2010), and the series edited by Robert G. Hoyland and Arietta Papaconstantinou, *The Worlds of Eastern Christianity, 300–1500* (Farnham: Ashgate, 2011–). See also for these issues in historiographical and hagiographical texts Arietta Papaconstantinou, with Muriel Debié and Hugh Kennedy, eds., *Writing "True Stories": Historians and Hagiographers in the Late antique and Medieval Near East* (Turnhout: Brepols, 2010). It is no surprise that the genesis of Arabic as a written language is currently a major (and obviously controversial) topic: for an introduction see Robert G. Hoyland, *Arabia and the Arabs. From the Bronze Age to the Coming of Islam* (London: Routledge, 2001).

37 Maijastina Kahlos, *Debate and Dialogue: Christian and Pagan Cultures c. 360–430* (Aldershot: Ashgate, 2007); ead., *Forbearance and Compulsion: The Rhetoric of Religious Tolerance and Intolerance in Late Antiquity* (London: Duckworth, 2009), ead., ed., *The Faces of the Other. Religious Rivalry and Ethnic Encounters in the Later Roman World* (Turnhout: Brepols, 2012).

an agenda, and recognition of this is, again, an example of an instrumentalist reading of Christian literature.

The instrumentalist reading feeds in to another highly prevalent idea, namely that of increasing Christian intolerance, a closing in of horizons in late antiquity.[38] On this view Christian literature contributed to an authoritarian atmosphere and fed in to a conflict model of religious life in late antiquity, which at times led to actual violence.[39] An extreme statement of the latter view can be found in Polymnia Athanassiadi's recent short book, *Vers la pensée unique* (2010), with its subtitle, *La montée de l'intolérance dans L'Antiquité tardive*.[40] Another version is contained in the quite widespread view that genuine debate was shut down some time in the fifth century, propounded in Richard Lim's otherwise excellent book of 1995, *Public Disputation, Power and Social Order in Late Antiquity*. Christian writing from then on was not free, if it had ever been, but existed to reinforce an authoritarian viewpoint.

Extreme as these views may sound, I cite them because they illustrate the general tendency to regard Christian writing as essentially functional – there for a purpose, that purpose being historical rather than literary, with literary issues regarded as serving the historical-theological purpose.

Against this dominant paradigm I want to set two other ways of approaching late antique Christian writing, and then to consider a specific example which may suggest some ways forward.

---

38 Cf. Graham Stanton and Guy G. Stroumsa, eds., *Tolerance and Intolerance in Early Judaism and Christianity* (Cambridge: Cambridge University Press, 2008); Averil Cameron, "Apologetics in the Roman empire – a genre of intolerance?," in *"Humana sapit". Études d'Antiquité tardive offertes à Lellia Cracco Ruggini*, eds. Jean-Michel Carrié and Rita Lizzi Testa, (Bibliothèque de l'Antiquité Tardive 3; Paris-Turnhout: Brepols, 2002): 219–227.
39 For the latter, Harold Drake, ed., *Violence in Late Antiquity: Perceptions and Practice* (Aldershot: Ashgate, 2006), with id., *Constantine and the Bishops. The Politics of Intolerance* (Baltimore, MD: Johns Hopkins University Press, 2000). A recent major research project led by Kate Cooper, with the title *Constantine's Dream*, asks the question whether monotheism inevitably leads to violence; a forthcoming conference in Finland at the time of writing announces its theme as "Conflict in Late Antiquity", including cultural, religious and doctrinal conflicts. In response to such recent emphases, others look for evidence of Christian tolerance: cf. Elizabeth DePalma Digeser, *The Making of a Christian Empire: Lactantius and Rome* (Ithaca, NY: Cornell University Press, 2000).
40 Athanassiadi's attack on Eusebius, for instance, and her highly-coloured emotive language in general have provoked an indignant response from Sébastien Morlet, "L'Antiquité tardive fut-elle une période d'obscurantisme?," *Adamantius* 16 (2010): 413–421.

4 Christian literature and rhetoric

The first of these other two ways of understanding Christian writing involves its relation to rhetoric. We have always known that rhetoric was the foundation of the educational system in the Roman empire and late antiquity and that rhetorical teaching had an enormous influence on the literature of the period. Educated Christians went to the same teachers and same schools as pagans, and often studied alongside them. There was no equivalent training in Christian theology, church history or teaching, and this formal rhetorical education necessarily shaped the way that Christians wrote.[41] As Peter Brown argues, and many before him, including of course Werner Jaeger,[42] *paideia* was fundamental to Christian success. In current scholarship rhetoric is enjoying a considerable amount of attention – the school of Libanius in Antioch, the teaching methods employed in Alexandria, the role of *grammatici* (the teachers of the first stage of education), and the rhetorical works, declamations and exercises by men like Libanius and Themistius have all been major topics.[43] How do Christian writers fit into this wider context?

One answer has been to propose that late antiquity enjoyed a "Third Sophistic" movement, on a par with the Second Sophistic in the early empire, and to allow at least some Christian writers a place within it.[44] Particular Christian writers who have been suggested for this role include Synesius of Cyrene, or the writers of the Gaza school in the early sixth century – Procopius and Choricius of

---

[41] Also Averil Cameron, "Education and literary culture," in *The Late Empire, AD 337–425*, eds., Averil Cameron and Peter Garnsey (Cambridge Ancient History XIII; Cambridge: Cambridge University Press, 1998), 665–707, at 675; see also Robert A. Kaster, "Education," in *Late Antiquity. A Guide to the Post-Classical World*, eds. Glen W. Bowersock, Peter R.L. Brown and Oleg Grabar (Cambridge, Massachusetts: Belknap Press of Harvard University Press, 1999): 421–423; Raffaella Cribiore, *Writing, Teachers and Students in Graeco-Roman Egypt* (Atlanta: Scholars Press, 1996); Catherine Chin, *Grammar and Christianity in the Late Roman World* (Philadelphia: University of Pennsylvania Press, 2008).
[42] Werner Jaeger, *Early Christianity and Greek Paideia* (Cambridge, Massachusetts: Belknap Press of Harvard University Press, 1961).
[43] Raffaella Cribiore, *The School of Libanius in Late Antique Antioch* (Princeton: Princeton University Press, 2007); ead., *Gymnastics of the Mind. Greek Education in Greek and Roman Egypt* (Princeton: Princeton University Press, 2001): 220–244; A. Quiroga Puertas, ed., *The Purpose of Rhetoric in Late Antiquity. From Performance to Exegesis* (Studies and Texts in Antiquity and Christianity 72; Tübingen: Mohr Siebeck, 2013).
[44] Averil Cameron, "Culture wars: late antiquity and literature," in *Libera Curiositas. Mélanges d'histoire romaine et d'Antiquité tardive offerts à Jean-Michel Carrié*, eds. C. Freu, S. Janniard and A. Ripoli (Bibliothèque de l'Antiquité Tardive 31; Paris, 2016).

Gaza. Methodius of Olympus, with his *Symposium*, clearly based on Plato's dialogue of the same name, is another possible candidate. But there are problems. For instance, the scholars who first propounded the idea of a Third Sophistic did not extend it to include Christian writers. Then again, while rhetoric was indeed a key component of the education many of them had received, only a few Christian authors themselves wrote the kinds of works that clearly fell into the category. The flourishing of rhetoric in late antiquity, whether or not it constituted a Third Sophistic, which is another matter, cannot be the main or only key to a critical analysis of Christian literature as a whole.

5 Christian literature and aesthetics

The second of the recent approaches that I mentioned, alongside the one that takes rhetoric as its starting point, is that of aesthetics. How far is it possible to approach Christian writing in late antiquity not in terms of its contribution to the historical development of Christianity but in terms of literary aesthetics, that is, as "literature"? This is new ground. To quote from Marco Formisano, "late antique literature nowadays represents not only a possible source of delight and 'pleasure' because of its novelty and freshness... but also the true worry for studies of the ancient world."[45] However, as Formisano also points out (510), the predominant hermeneutic is still historical or classicizing, and the aesthetics of late antique literature itself, not just Christian writing, are only just beginning to be addressed. I am also struck by the fact that many of the relevant works focus on Latin rather than Greek, perhaps because Latinists have had to grapple with particularly entrenched conceptions of an existential "conflict" between paganism

---

[45] Marco Formisano, "Late antiquity: new departures," in *The Oxford Handbook of Medieval Latin Literature*, eds. Ralph J. Hexter and David Townsend (Oxford: Oxford University Press, 2012): 509–534, at 509, citing also Danuta Shanzer, "Literature, history, periodization and the pleasures of the Latin literary history of late antiquity," *History Compass* 7 (2009): 917–954.

and Christianity.[46] They also, perhaps predictably, tend to focus on poetry.[47] Part of the impetus behind this work is the wish to rescue late antique literature from the stigma of "decline". It necessarily, if sometimes problematically, includes Christian as well as secular writing. It thus risks collapsing the category 'Christian' into that of 'late antique'. But equally, it has the advantage that Christian literature comes out of its special box, and can be viewed simply as "literature".[48] Suggested general tendencies said to be manifested in the literature of late antiquity include a rise in collections,[49] commentary (incorporating exegesis), epideictic (including biography, saints' lives and other works), visuality and fragmentation.[50] The functional aspects of Christian writing are not the focus here. Quite the

---

46 Amply documented and discussed by Alan Cameron, *Last Pagans*; however, the level of emotion evidently attached to these issues by some scholars is revealed in Stéphane Ratti, "Païens et chrétiens en IVe siècle: points de résistance à une *doxa*," *Antiquité tardive* 21 (2013): 401–410, where Ratti supports Athanassiadi, *Vers la pensée unique* against the position of Alan Cameron, which he identifies with that of Peter Brown; see also S. Ratti and Jean-Michel Carrié, *Antiquus Error. Les ultimes feux de la résistance païenne. Scripta varia augmentés de cinq études inédites*, Bibliothèque de l'Antiquité Tardive 14 (Turnhout: Brepols, 2010); id., *Polémique entre païens et chrétiens* (Paris: Les Belles Letrres, 2012); *The Strange Death of Pagan Rome. Reflections on a Historical Controversy*, ed. Rita Lizzi-Testa (Turnhout: Brepols, 2014).
47 Michael Roberts, *The Jeweled Style. Poetry and Poetics in Late Antiquity* (Ithaca, NY: Cornell University Press, 1989); Patricia Cox Miller, *The Poetry of Thought in Late Antiquity. Essays in Imagination and Religion* (Aldershot: Ashgate, 2001); Juan Hernández Lobato, *Vel Apolline muto. Estética y Poetica de la Antigüedad tardia* (Bern: Peter Lang, 2012), on Sidonius Apollinaris, with Joop A. van Warden and Gavin Kelly, eds., *New Approaches to Sidonius Apollinaris* (Leuven: Peeters, 2013); some relevant contributions in Helmut Seng and Lars M. Hoffmann, eds., *Synesios von Kyrene. Politik – Literatur – Philosophie* (Turnhout: Brepols, 2012); Marco Formisano, "Towards an aesthetic paradigm of late antiquity," *Antiquité tardive* 15 (2007): 277–284; Scott Fitzgerald Johnson, ed., *Greek Literature in Late Antiquity: Dynamism, Didacticism, Classicism* (Aldershot: Ashgate, 2006); John H.D. Scourfield, ed., *Texts and Culture in Late Antiquity. Inheritance, Authority and Change* (Swansea: Classical Press of Wales, 2007); Mary Whitby, "Writing in Greek: classicism and compilation, interaction and transformation", in *Theodosius II: Rethinking the Roman Empire in Late Antiquity*, ed. Christopher Kelly (Cambridge: Cambridge University Press, 2013), 195–218, and compare also the works by Mark Vessey already cited.
48 Compare the similar changes of perception that have already affected the category of "Christian archaeology".
49 See Claudio Moreschini, ed., *Esegesi, parafrasi e compilazione in età tardoantica* (Atti del terzo convegno dell'Associazione di Studi Tardoantichi, Collectanea 9; Naples: M. D'Auria, 1995).
50 Formisano, "Late antiquity: new departures"; cf. 518, the point of commentary being to make new; cf. 519, Christian literature as inherently intertextual; also John H.D. Scourfield, "Textual inheritances and textual relations in late antiquity," in Scourfield, ed., *Texts and Culture in Late Antiquity*, 1–32, at 16 and 19.

opposite. Rather than argue for Christian writing as constitutive of a late antique Christian world, the literary approach takes late antique literature, including Christian literature, as a *reflection* of contemporary society.

6 Christian literature and faith

The two approaches to Christian writing that I have outlined focus on it either as essentially formative of Christian society, or as a cultural phenomenon reflective of society itself. They differ fundamentally from each other. But in both cases most of the scholars in question are scholars of late antiquity, not church historians or theologians. One could say indeed that both ways of interpretation represent a takeover of patristics by scholars of late antiquity. A third, and again fundamentally different approach, is illustrated in the very recent book by Frances Young, *God's Presence*,[51] which is deliberately cast as a theological and very personal engagement with the Fathers. Very remarkably, she describes and defends her methods and her aims as "a contemporary recapitulation of early Christianity", an engagement with the Fathers in terms of modern concerns such as science, evolution and gender, and so a conversation with Basil, the Gregorys, Augustine and others in which she shows how their concerns and their arguments, which seem so very different from ours, are really addressing issues still, and no doubt always, current. But then, she is not addressing the Fathers as writers but as theologians. What we see, in sharp contrast, in much of the other current work on Christian writers in late antiquity, explicitly or not, is, as I said earlier, the reduction of this field to that of cultural studies, an approach which necessarily implies a rather selective choice of texts to discuss. Is this, in the English phrase, throwing out the baby with the bathwater? And further, in terms of the study of religion, rather than of theology as such, what does it tell us about current definitions of culture and the place of religion within it? It has been said that late antiquity was above all logocentric. The linguistic turn, and the current emphasis on discourse analysis in relation to early Christian writing have been enormously productive. Yet it does seem to me that there are questions that they cannot answer.

---

51 Frances M. Young, *God's Presence. A Contemporary Recapitulation of Early Christianity* (Cambridge: Cambridge University Press, 2013).

7 An example: Christian prose dialogues

In the remainder of this lecture I want to take one example of early Christian writing which illustrates some of these issues. This is the example of Christian prose dialogues. These begin early, with writers like Justin Martyr and in Latin Minucius Felix, and they continue in Greek not only in late antiquity but also throughout the Byzantine period and even later. In the course of current research, and with the help of two excellent assistants, I have compiled a very long list of such works, not including most of the related but mostly dissimilar examples of *erotapokriseis* or questions and answers, on which others are working.[52] One of the principal results of my inquiries is the realisation of just how varied these dialogues could be.[53] They range from the highly literary, and Platonising, to the more functional. Some are more "dialogic", others contain long speeches in favour of a particular argument, with only a nod towards characterization or scene-setting.[54] The titles in the MSS and those traditionally given in the secondary literature range over several different terms – *dialogos, disputatio, dialexis* and others – and are not necessarily reliable guides to the nature of an individual work; it is better at this stage therefore to avoid generalizations about genre or literary form. It has been argued recently by Richard Lim and especially by Simon Goldhill that "true dialogue", that is, unbiased discussion according to current ideas of what dialogue should be, ended with the advance of Christianity.[55] They place this break sometime in the fifth century. This is of course a version of the idea that Christianity brought intolerance, and that Christian literature can therefore only

---

[52] Annelie Volgers and Claudio Zamagni, eds., *Erotapokriseis: Early Christian Question and Answer Literature in Context* (Leuven: Peeters, 2004); Marie-Pierre Bussières, ed., *La littérature des questions et réponses dans l'Antiquité profane et chrétienne : de l'enseignement à l'exégèse : actes du séminaire sur le genre des questions et réponses tenu à Ottawa les 27 et 28 septembre 2009* (Instrumenta Patristica et Mediaevalia 64; Turnhout: Brepols, 2013). Question-and-answer collections are also the central subject of a major research project led by Ioannis Papadogiannakis at King's College London. However, it must be admitted that it is becoming increasingly clear that the boundaries between these groups of literary works are often very blurred.
[53] Averil Cameron, "Can Christians do dialogue?," *Studia Patristica* 63.11 (2013): 103–120; ead., *Dialog und Debatte in der Spätantike*.
[54] Vittorio Hösle, *Der philosophische Dialog: eine Poetik und Hermeneutik* (München: C.H. Beck, 2006) does not consider the very large number of dialogues from the Byzantine period.
[55] Richard Lim, *Public Disputation, Power and Social Order in Late Antiquity* (Berkeley: University of California Press, 1995); Simon Goldhill, ed., *The End of Dialogue in Antiquity* (Cambridge: Cambridge University Press, 2009), Introduction; Daniel Boyarin, "Dialectic and Divination in the Talmud," ibid., 217–241.

be one-sided. A rather different argument emphasizes a desire for consensus and accepts the idea that by the end of late antiquity the state did indeed impose a kind of uniformity of thought and expression; formal discussions were useful ways of reaching such consensus.[56]

Since argumentation and its various techniques were at a such premium for Christians, especially in the context of ecclesiastical synods and councils, the nature of the argumentation in accounts of debates and in prose dialogue writing by Christians is surely an issue of key importance. In fact the extraordinary vitality of this way of writing, that is, of writing dialogues, seems to me absolutely to contradict the claims made by Goldhill and others. I believe that a long view is also essential, and for the Greek dialogues ideally one that encompasses the Byzantine period as well as the late antique. Finally, I am convinced that in such an enquiry one should include the better-known but also highly relevant corpora of Christian-Jewish and later Christian-Muslim dialogues, each of which has its own large secondary literature, usually without reference to the much wider and more varied body of dialogue writing on other subjects.[57]

The questions that arise from such an inquiry are many, and some of them have been unexpected. For instance, in what critical terms should Christian prose dialogues be approached? Are they to be seen as literary works, pieces of polemic, or catechetical exercises? Rhetoric can hardly be irrelevant; after all, students were trained in argument, and in imaginary disputes, as well as in *ethopoiia*, characterization. Yet the rhetorical handbooks do not prescribe exercises for writing dialogues, and when one does come across statements about them, they are classified not in terms of *eloquentia* but of *sermocinatio* – the conversational rather than the rhetorical style. Lucian's satirical dialogue known as the *Bis accusatus* depicts Lucian himself ("the Syrian") being put on trial for deserting rhetoric for dialogue. Rhetoric (oratory) accuses him of rejecting her and following instead a bearded old person, namely Dialogue, who claims to be the son of Philosophy. Instead of thundering oratory, says Rhetoric, he can only use short paragraphs in conversational style.[58] The literary manner assumed to be appropriate for dialogue, unlike the rhetorical style of oratory, is "relaxed", or '"informal",

---

56 Peter Van Nuffelen, "The end of open competition? Religious disputations in late antiquity," in Engels and Van Nuffelen, eds. *Competition and Religion in Antiquity*, 149–172.
57 In the case of the former, recent contributions are increasingly demonstrating the permeability between the *Adversus Iudaeos* literature and other kinds of patristic writing: see some of the papers in Sébastien Morlet, Olivier Munnich, Bernard Pouderon, eds., *Les dialogues* Adversus Iudaeos. *Permanences et mutations d'une tradition polémique* (Paris: Institut d'études augustiniennes, 2013).
58 Lucian, *Bis accusatus* 28 (BSGRT *Lucianus Opera* 3, 20 Jacobitz).

the style of conversation, as Cyril of Alexandria also explains in the preface to his seven dialogues on the Trinity, and as is specified in the influential treatise of Demetrius, *On Style*.[59]

Lucian's reference to philosophy raises a further issue. A fair proportion of Christian dialogues begin (even if they do not carry it on through the rest of the work) with a Platonizing setting, which is sometimes based on the opening of Plato's *Republic*, or on the *Phaedrus* or *Phaedo*, or the *Protagoras*. Not many are as philosophical or as indebted to Plato in content as Gregory of Nyssa's *De Anima*, or *On the Soul*. But the sixth-century dialogue on the eternity of the world known as the *Ammonius* by Zacharias Scholasticus (actually a set of dialogues) is set in the lecture room of the Alexandrian philosopher, Neoplatonist and Aristotelian commentator Ammonius, during lectures on the *Physics* and the *Ethics* – possibly in one of the very classrooms now excavated and published by Polish archaeologists.[60] The influence of Plato on early Christianity is not something I need to argue here;[61] moreover, it increasingly seems that philosophy and rhetoric were not completely separate in late antique education. But I have also observed the influence of Aristotle becoming more and more evident in the late antique dialogues, some of which are also much more technical in their argumentation. The latter feature is connected with the increased premium placed on proof texts and technical argument, as the individual and collective stakes rose higher and higher for Christians in doctrinal competition, but it must also be connected with the continuous teaching of Aristotle's logic during late antiquity and Byzantium. That is certainly also the case with the writings of the east Syrians associated with the School of Nisibis.[62] In the Byzantine period the trend expresses itself in the practice of appending lists of syllogisms to the dialogues, by way of reinforcing the argument. Plato on the other hand was not a regular part

---

59 Cyril of Alexandria, *Dialogues on the Trinity, Praefatio* (SC 231, 128,3–5 Durand); Demetrius, *On Style* 19–21 (William R. Roberts, ed., *Demetrius on Style* [Cambridge: Cambridge University Press, 1902], 79).
60 T. Derda et al., eds., *Alexandria: Auditoria of Kom el-Dikka and Late Antique Education* (Journal of Juristic Papyrology Supplement 8; Warsaw: David Brown Book Company, 2007).
61 Scourfield, "Textual inheritances and textual relations in late antiquity", 21–22.
62 Adam H. Becker, *Fear of God and the Beginning of Wisdom. The School of Nisibis and the Development of Scholastic Culture in Late Antique Mesopotamia* (Philadelphia: University of Pennsyvania Press, 2006); the same is argued for the west Syrian Miaphysites by Jack Tannous, *Syria between Byzantium and Islam: Making Incommensurables Speak* (PhD diss. Princeton, 2010), and see id., "'You are what you read': Qenneshre and the Miaphysite church in the seventh century," in *History and Identity in the Late Antique Near East*, ed. Philip Wood (Oxford: Oxford University Press, 2010), 83–102.

of the Byzantine curriculum in the same way, and indeed became highly suspect as the source of dangerously pagan teachings. Yet writers of dialogues in later Byzantium also continued to give their works a Platonizing setting. To take a different example from a much earlier period, recent work on Plutarch's dialogues has sought to rehabilitate his genuinely philosophical purpose.[63] I believe that investigating some of the Christian dialogues in the same way would be very fruitful. They belong to the history of philosophy as well as to those of literature and of course theology.[64] These works, written by Christians of many different types and at different intellectual levels, are an important part of the intellectual as well as the Christian history of late antiquity and the Byzantine period, though their importance for the latter is as yet barely recognized.[65]

Some of the dialogues, for instance Augustine's debates with Manichaeans, claim to be the records of real debates. In some cases this may be clear enough, though we are not in a position to know how faithfully the written version reflects what was actually said, and how far such claims can be believed is often hard to establish, even though there was certainly a thick context of public debates in late antiquity,[66] we know that public debate was indeed a feature of the culture of late antiquity, and staged religious discussions frequently took place.[67] The question of whether the literary dialogues reflect actual encounters remains a particular concern in much of the literature on the anti-Jewish dialogues, driven by the longstanding aim of trying to discern the nature of actual Christian and Jewish relations and the extent of the Jewish presence during the early centuries of Christianity.[68] The problem is often couched in terms of having to choose between positing a real debate and supposing that the dialogue was composed for

---

[63] See for instance Frieda Klotz and Aikaterini Oikonomopoulou, eds., *The Philosopher's Banquet. Plutarch's 'Table Talk' in the Intellectual Context of the Roman Empire* (Oxford: Oxford University Press, 2011).
[64] The philosophical element in Christian literature is also brought out in Ryan C. Fowler, ed., *Plato in the Third Sophistic* (Berlin: De Gruyter, 2013).
[65] Theological dialogues are dismissed as unimportant by Paul Magdalino, *The Empire of Manuel I Komnenos 1143–1180* (Cambridge: Cambridge University Press, 1993), 367 ("derivative in the extreme").
[66] See Averil Cameron, *Dialog und Debatte in der Spätantike*, Kap. 2.
[67] Hubert Cancik, "Antike Religionsgespräche," in *Medien religiöser Kommunikationen im Imperium Romanum*, eds. Günther Schörner and Darja Erker Sterbenc (Potsdamer Altertumswissenschaftliche Beiträge 24; Stuttgart: Steiner, 2008): 15–25.
[68] See for instance L. Lahey, "Evidence for Jewish believers in Christian-Jewish dialogues through the sixth century (excluding Justin)," in *Jewish Believers in Jesus: the Early Centuries*, ed. O. Skarsaune (Peabody, Mass.: Hendrickson, 2007): 581–639; id., "Jewish biblical interpretation

catechetical purposes, but this is to over-simplify what is in fact a complex range of possibilities, and effectively to deny this category of Christian writing a place within the overall corpus of Christian literary production.

According to Goldhill, Christian dialogues were by their very nature closed: they were designed to put a case, to demolish the opposition, and there could be only one conclusion. But besides relying on a somewhat idealized view of supposedly "democratic" Platonic dialogues in classical Athens,[69] this completely fails to appreciate the plurality of Christian voices and opinions in late antiquity. A "cacophony" of voices is a better description, perhaps.[70] I will argue elsewhere that this intense argumentation continued even in Byzantium, which is usually still written off as stiflingly Orthodox.[71] As for literary dialogues, they enjoyed a remarkable efflorescence in late Byzantium, which I hope to discuss further.

8 Conclusion

I hope to have pointed in this lecture to several current discussions that are going on about Christian literature. The great difference between the scholars engaging in these and Lietzmann himself is that these debates are now being conducted not by church historians so much as by scholars of late antiquity, who have in a sense appropriated the territory. Behind the current disagreements are historical questions, for instance about the periodization of late antiquity, and certainly about Christianization. This partly accounts for the evident differences between those who concentrate on late Latin literature (from the part of the Roman empire that arguably ended earlier) and those who work on the east. A further historical question lies behind much current writing, namely whether late antiquity was

---

and genuine Jewish-Christian debate in the dialogue of Timothy and Aquila," *Journal of Jewish Studies* 51.2 (2000): 281–296.
69 Forcefully denied recently by Daniel Boyarin, *Socrates and the Fat Rabbis* (Chicago: Chicago University Press, 2009).
70 The term is used by Andrew Jacobs of some kinds of early Christian writing in Andrew S. Jacobs, "Dialogical differences: (De-)Judaizing Jesus' circumcision," *Journal of Early Christian Studies* 15 (2007): 291–335, at 329, as providing "a space for the dialogic cacophony of different voices even as they were ostensibly refining and narrowing the bounds of 'orthodox' identity".
71 For assertion of an "Orthodox culture", at least after the ending of Byzantine iconoclasm in AD 843, see Paul Magdalino, "Orthodoxy and Byzantine cultural identity," in *Orthodoxy and Heresy in Byzantium: The Definition and the Notion of Orthodoxy and Some Other Studies on the Heresies and the Non-Christian Religions*, eds. Antonio Rigo and Pavel Ermilov (Quaderni di *Nea Rhome* 4; Rome: Università degli studi di Roma "Tor Vergata", 2010): 21–46.

intolerant (and violent) – itself a reaction against the "benign'" late antiquity of Peter Brown and indeed of myself in an earlier incarnation. The notion of an intolerant Christian late antiquity is also connected with the assumption (to echo Lim and Goldhill again) that somehow everything was then settled, with a stifling of debate and a general climate of repression. The longer timescale that I invoke undercuts this idea and enables us to continue to study Christian writing in later periods with a more open mind.

As Frances Young and others have remarked, we are still mainly in the context of historical readings of late antique Christian literature. Fergus Millar for example interprets the *Life of Symeon the Stylite the Younger* (not the earlier Symeon the Stylite of Hans Lietzmann) in terms of what it can tell us about Syriac language and culture in the late sixth century.[72] The instrumentalist reading of late antique Christian writing that I have described also deduces historical conclusions from literary texts. Neither approach is the approach of a theologian, or even of a church historian, Indeed, church history itself has to some extent been collapsed into this general cultural model of late antiquity, from which, needless to say, confessional history is equally absent. Against this, a few scholars are asking a different question altogether: how we might address and evaluate this very large body of writing in literary, rather than historical terms. These approaches, as Mark Vessey's work demonstrates, are still in their infancy. Perhaps this is not the right question, but I believe it needs to be asked.

If we are really in a period when the analysis of Christian literature is not only a source of pleasure (*jouissance*) but "the true worry for studies of the ancient world" (Formisano), I can only rejoice that new questions are being asked and perhaps new solutions found for understanding the enormous, challenging and often still unstudied repertoire of Christian writing. If this means that scholars from other disciplines are occupying territory that would once have been that of a church historian, that may have its own dangers. But it cannot be altogether a bad thing, even if they do not share all the aims and assumptions that our predecessors like Hans Lietzmann once brought to the subject.

---

[72] Fergus Millar, "The image of a Christian monk in northern Syria: Symeon Stylites the Younger," in *Being Christian in Late Antiquity: A Festschrift for Gillian Clark*, eds. Carol Harrison, Caroline Humfress and Isabella Sandwell (Oxford: Oxford University Press, 2014): 278–295.